GW01281579

33

16

47

INTRODUCTION

Bangkok is one of the most exciting and dynamic cities in Southeast Asia. Double-digit economic growth during the 1980s and 1990s brought air-conditioned shopping malls, elevated and underground urban railways and world-class architectural experiments. A severe recession in the late 1990s nearly halted the economy but prompted an inwardly focused artistic renaissance that included critically hailed Thai new-wave cinema and an explosion of independent music. Recent years have seen social unrest and mass demonstrations, with some tourists left stranded in 2008 when the city's airports were occupied by protestors. Despite these troubles Bangkok continues to lure curious visitors from around the world with its unique blend of the spiritual, carnal and entrepreneurial.

A Distinctive Capital

Straddling the Chao Phraya River delta, metropolitan Bangkok covers 1,569 sq km (606 sq miles) and sprawls into the neighbouring provinces of Nonthaburi, Samut Prakan and Samut Sakhon. The rivers and tributaries of northern and central Thailand drain into the Chao Phraya River, which in turn disgorges into the Gulf of Thailand, a vast cul-de-sac of the South China Sea only a few kilometres from central Bangkok.

The capital is surrounded on three sides by a huge, wet, flat and extremely fertile area known as 'the rice bowl of Asia' – more rice is grown here than in any other area of comparable size in all of Asia. Thailand has, in fact, been the world's top exporter of rice for at least the last 30 years. A vast spider web of natural and artificial canals fan out through this sultry river delta for several hundred square kilometres. Criss-

Thai *lakhon* dancers in traditional costume

crossing the city in all directions, these murky green waterways conjure up a parallel universe in which 18th-century Siam collides with 21st-century Thailand.

The capital is administered as a separate province, and has the only elected governorship in the nation (other provincial governors are appointed by the ministry). Press freedoms envied by neighbouring nations have made Bangkok Asia's largest base for foreign media correspondents. As a primary gateway for investment in neighbouring Vietnam, Cambodia, Laos and Myanmar, the city also serves as a financial hub for mainland Southeast Asia.

Banking, finance, wholesale and retail trade, transport, tourism and energy dominate the immediate municipality, while the surrounding metropolitan area adds manufacturing, shipping, food processing and intensive farming to the list of top revenue producers. Per capita income in metropolitan Bangkok runs well above the average in the rest of the country.

Figures on Bangkok's infamous nightlife-based economy are difficult to come by, and civic leaders prefer to keep it that way. When Longman's *Dictionary of Contemporary English* defined Bangkok as 'a place where there are a lot of prostitutes', Thais filed diplomatic protests and staged demonstrations outside the British Embassy. Longman agreed to withdraw the offending edition from circulation, although the blunder was echoed a few years later when Microsoft's *Encarta* labelled Bangkok as a 'commercial sex hub', resulting in a lawsuit and subsequent revision of the entry.

At the floating market

Population

Official estimates place metropolitan Bangkok's population at 8 million, though some claim this figure may be as much as 7 million short as the city has many unregistered residents. An astonishing 5,000 residents compete for every square kilometre, propelling a creative turbine that never ceases as the city's past and future co-evolve, from farms to freeways, spirit shrines to art galleries. Visitors won't be surprised to hear that one in eight Thais lives in Bangkok, or that 60 percent of the country's wealth is concentrated here.

Built-up Bangkok

Only a little over half of the city's inhabitants are ethnic Thais, with Thai as their first language. Although Thais are found in all walks of life, they are the backbone of Bangkok's blue-collar workforce, construction, automotive repair and river transport.

Up to 25 percent of the city's population is of Chinese or mixed Thai and Chinese descent. Many Bangkok Chinese-Thais speak both Thai and a Chinese dialect, such as Cantonese, Hokkien or Chiu Chau. Chinese influence is so strong that in certain areas of the city – such as Yaowarat, Bangkok's Chinatown, or Pathumwan, the city's wealthiest precinct – you can almost imagine you're in Hong Kong or Singapore rather than Thailand. In these areas Chinese tend to be engaged in all manner of commerce, from wholesale trade in auto parts to the manufacture of high-end kitchen utensils. In other parts of the city they dominate higher education, international trade, banking and white-collar employment in general.

Bangkok's second-largest Asian minority claims South Asian descent, most tracing their heritage to northern India, including many Sikhs who immigrated during the 1947 Partition of India. Many of the city's South Asians can be found in a neighbourhood known as Phahurat (off the northern end of Yaowarat Road, between Chakraphet and Phahurat roads), or in Bangrak (along Charoen Krung Road, near junctions with Silom and Surawong roads). In both areas they operate a multitude of successful retail businesses, particularly textile and tailor shops.

Buddhas in Wat Suthat

People from the Middle East probably reached Thailand before most other ethnic groups, including the Thais themselves, having traded along the Thai coastlines in the early years of the first Christian millennium. The first global oil crisis in the 1970s saw a renewal of Arab business interests in Bangkok, and today the area known as Nana, roughly extending from Soi 3 to Soi 11 along Sukhumvit Road, sees a high concentration of both residents and tourists from the Middle East.

Bangkok's residents of European descent number around 45,000. The vast majority, unlike their Asian counterparts, find themselves in Thailand for only a few months or years for reasons of work or study. As a reflection of their countries' significant roles in the early development of Bangkok, residents of German and British descent appear to be most prominent.

Religion

Around 92 percent of Bangkokians follow Theravada Buddhism, the world's oldest

Young novice monks

and most traditional Buddhist sect. Walk the streets of Bangkok early in the morning and you'll catch rows of shaved heads bobbing above bright ochre robes, as monks all over the city engage in the daily house-to-house alms-food-gathering. Thai men are expected to don monastic robes temporarily at least once in their lives. Some enter the monkhood twice, first as 10-vow novices in their pre-teen years and then as fully ordained, 227-vow monks some time after the age of 20.

Thai Buddhists believe that individuals work out their own paths to *nibbana* (nirvana) through a combination of good works, meditation and study of the *dhamma* or Buddhist philosophy. The presence of *wats* (monasteries) scattered around the city serves as a reminder that Buddhism retains a certain dominance even in increasingly secular Bangkok.

Green-hued onion domes looming over rooftops belong to mosques and mark the immediate neighbourhood as Muslim, while brightly painted and ornately carved cement spires indicate a Hindu temple. Wander down congested Chakraphet

What's a *wat*?

Bangkok has over 300 Buddhist monasteries (*wat* in Thai), each consisting of a walled compound containing several buildings constructed in the traditional Thai style with steep, swooping rooflines and colourful interior murals.

Road in the Phahurat district to find Sri Gurusingh Sabha, a Sikh temple where visitors are welcome. A handful of steepled Christian churches, some of them historic, have taken root over the centuries and can be found near the banks of the Chao Phraya River. In Chinatown large round doorways topped with heavily inscribed Chinese characters and flanked by red paper lanterns denote *san jao*, Chinese temples dedicated to the worship of Buddhist, Taoist and Confucian deities.

Something for Everyone

As varied as it is vast, Bangkok offers residents and visitors alike the assurance they will never be bored. One can move across the city on water via 18th-century canals, in the air aboard the sleek Skytrain or below ground in the high-tech Metropolitan Rapid Transit Authority (MRTA) subway. When hunger beckons, residents are spoiled by a panoply of the finest Thai restaurants anywhere in the kingdom, along with a host of other Asian cuisines and a broad range of European fare prepared by native chefs. Night falls and one can attend a classical Thai masked dance-drama performance followed by a club jaunt to hear a visiting DJ spin the latest house music. One of Asia's best-kept secrets when it comes to shopping, the city offers everything from custom-tailored suits to Asian antiques at prices no other Asian capital can rival.

Bangkok also serves as a convenient base for excursions to Nakhon Pathom (location of Thailand's largest Buddhist *stupa*, or monument), Kanchanaburi (Bridge on the River Kwai), Ayuthaya and the island of Ko Samet.

A BRIEF HISTORY

Founded barely 200 years ago, Bangkok can't claim an ancient pedigree. Yet its relatively brief history sees the transformation of a small river-bank trading village into Southeast Asia's most dynamic and colourful capital.

Bangkok's Predecessor

Bangkok's political and cultural identity originally took shape 86km (53 miles) upriver in Ayuthaya, the royal capital of Siam – as Thailand was then known – from 1350 to 1767. Encircled by rivers with access to the Gulf of Thailand, Ayuthaya flourished as a sea port courted by Dutch, Portuguese, French, English, Chinese and Japanese merchants. By the end of the 17th century, Ayuthaya had a population of 1 million and was one of the wealthiest and most powerful cities in Asia.

Wat Phra Si Sanphet, Ayuthaya

Throughout four centuries of Ayuthaya reign, several European powers tried without success to establish colonial relationships with the kingdom of Siam. A Burmese army finally subdued the capital in 1767, destroying most of Ayuthaya's Buddhist temples and royal edifices.

Founding a New Capital

Four years after this devastating defeat, the Siamese re-grouped under Phaya Taksin, a half-Chinese, half-Thai general who decided to move the capital further south along Chao Phraya River, closer to the Gulf of Siam. Thonburi Si Mahasamut, founded 200 years earlier by a group of wealthy Thais who had turned it into an important trade entrepôt during the height of Ayuthaya's power, was a logical choice.

Fearing Thailand was vulnerable to further Burmese attacks from the west, in 1782 Taksin's successor Phaya Chakri moved the capital across the river to a smaller settlement known as Bang Makok, after the *makok* (olive plum) trees which grew there in abundance. As the first monarch of the new Chakri royal dynasty – which continues to this day – Phaya Chakri was later dubbed King Rama I.

Under Rama I, the Siamese erected a new royal palace, raised 10km (6 miles) of city walls and dug a system of canals to create a moated, royal 'island' known as Ko Rattanakosin. Sections of the 4.5m (15ft) thick walls can still be seen near

River Re-Routing

One of the city's major physical transformations occurred in the late 18th century with the digging of a canal to create a short cut across a large bend in the Chao Phraya River, thus hastening water transport to the north.

The Chao Phraya's original river course along that bend gradually diverted much of its volume to the canal short cut. Today, most visitors and residents are unaware that the section of river running along the immediate west of Ko Rattanakosin is technically an artificial canal. Meanwhile, the original river loop, nowadays assumed to be a *khlong* (canal), has taken on the name of Khlong Bangkok Noi.

Wat Saket and the Golden Mount, and along the Chao Phraya River. The canal-moats still flow, albeit sluggishly, around the original royal district.

Craftsmen who had survived the sacking of Ayuthaya built several magnificent temples and royal administrative buildings for the new capital. In 1785, the city was given a new name: *Krungthep mahanakhon bowon rattanakosin mahintara ayuthaya mahadilok popnop-*

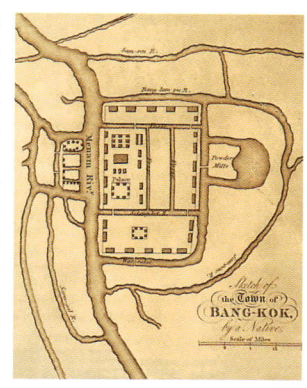

Early waterway map

parat ratchathani burirom udomratchaniwet mahasathan amonpima avatansathir sakkathatitya visnukamprasit. The name translates as 'Great city of angels, the repository of divine gems, the great land unconquerable, the grand and prominent realm, the royal and delightful capital city full of nine noble gems, the highest royal dwelling and grand palace, the divine shelter and living place of reincarnated spirits'.

Foreign traders continued to call the capital Bang Makok, which eventually truncated itself to 'Bangkok', the name most commonly known to the outside world today. The Thais, meanwhile, commonly use a shortened version of the given name, Krung Thep (City of Angels).

Kings Rama II and Rama III ordered the building of more temples, and the system of rivers, streams and natural canals surrounding the capital was augmented by the excavation of additional waterways.

Water-borne traffic dominated the city, supplemented by a meagre network of footpaths, well into the middle of the

The Grand Palace is a blend of Thai and Western architecture

19th century. In response to requests from diplomats and international merchants, Rama IV (King Mongkut, 1851–68) established a handful of roadways suitable for horse-drawn carriages and rickshaws in the mid-1800s. The first – and most ambitious road project for nearly a century to come – was Charoen Krung Road (also known by its English name, New Road), which ran 10km (6 miles) south from Wat Pho along the east bank of the Chao Phraya River. This swathe of hand-laid cobblestone, which took four years to finish, eventually accommodated a tramway as well as early automobiles.

His successor Rama V (King Chulalongkorn, 1868–1910) added the much wider Ratchadamnoen Klang Road to provide a suitably royal promenade – modelled after the Champs-Elysées and lined with ornamental gardens – between the Grand Palace and the expanding commercial centre to the east of Ko Rattanakosin.

Despite its modest size, the capital administered the much larger kingdom of Siam – which extended well into parts of what are today Laos, Cambodia and Malaysia – quite well. Even more impressive, Siamese rulers were able to stave off steady and at times intense pressure from the Portuguese, the Dutch, the French and the English, all of whom at one time or another wanted to add Siam to their colonial portfolios. By the end of the 19th century, France and England had established imperial rule in every one of Siam's neighbouring countries – the French in Indochina and the English in Burma and Malaya.

Revolution, Coup and Counter-Coup

In 1924, a handful of Thai students in Paris formed a group that met to discuss ideas for a future Siamese government modelled on Western democracy. After finishing their studies and returning to Bangkok, three of these students – lawyer Pridi Banomyong and military officers Phibul Songkhram and Prayoon Phamonmontri – organised an underground 'People's

International Influence

Bangkok's ability to maintain Siam's independence meant that the kingdom was free to draw upon the talents of any architect or transport developer in the world, a freedom that helps explain the enormous variety – both planned and unplanned – in the capital today.

Germans were hired to design and build railways emanating from the capital, while the Dutch contributed Bangkok's central railway station, today considered a minor masterpiece of civic Art Deco. Americans established Siam's first printing press along with the kingdom's first newspaper in 1844. The first Thai-language newspaper, *Darunovadha*, came along in 1874, and by 1900 Bangkok had three daily English-language newspapers, the *Bangkok Times*, *Siam Observer* and *Siam Free Press*.

Royal Barges for Rama VII's coronation, 1925

Party' dedicated to the overthrow of the Siamese system of government. The People's Party found a willing accomplice in Rama VII, and a bloodless revolution in 1932 transformed Thailand from an absolute monarchy into a constitutional one.

Phibul Songkhram, appointed prime minister by the People's Party in December 1938, changed the country's name from Siam to Thailand and introduced the Western solar calendar. When the Japanese invaded Southeast Asia in 1941, outflanking Allied troops in Malaya and Burma, Phibul allowed them access to the Gulf of Thailand. Japanese troops bombed and briefly occupied parts of Bangkok on their way to the Thai-Burmese border to fight the British in Burma and, as a result of public insecurity, the Thai economy stagnated.

Phibul resigned in 1944 under pressure from the Thai underground resistance, and after VJ Day in 1945 was exiled to Japan. After three years, Phibul returned to Thailand and took over the leadership again via a military coup. Over the next 15 years, bridges were built over Mae Nam Chao Phraya, canals were filled in to provide space for new roads, and multi-storey buildings began crowding out traditional teak structures.

Another coup installed Field Marshal Sarit Thanarat in 1957, only to be deposed in 1964 by Thai army officers Thanom Kittikachorn and Praphat Charusathien, who ruled Thailand for nine years, allowing the US to establish several army bases within Thai borders to support the US campaign in Indochina. During this time Bangkok gained notoriety as a 'rest and recreation' (R&R) spot for foreign troops stationed in Southeast Asia.

In October 1973, the Thai military brutally suppressed a large pro-democracy student demonstration at Thammasat University in Bangkok, but King Bhumibol and General Krit Sivara, who sympathised with the students, refused to support further bloodshed, forcing Thanom and Praphat out. Oxford-educated leftist Kukrit Pramoj took charge of a 14-party coalition government and ejected the US military forces.

The Thai military regained control in 1976 after right-wing paramilitary groups assaulted a group of 2,000 students holding a sit-in at Thammasat, killing hundreds. Many students fled Bangkok and joined the People's Liberation Army of Thailand (PLAT), an armed Communist insurgency based in the hills since the 1930s.

Although a 1982 amnesty brought an end to PLAT, and students, workers and farmers returned to their homes, a new era of political tolerance exposed the military once again to civilian fire. In May 1992, several huge demonstrations demanding the resignation of the latest dictator, General Suchinda Kraprayoon, rocked Bangkok and the large provincial capitals. Bangkok governor Chamlong Srimuang, winner of the 1992 Magsaysay Award (a humanitarian service award issued in the Philippines) for his role in galvanising the public to reject Suchinda, led the protests. After confrontations between the protesters and the military near the Democracy Monument resulted in nearly 50 deaths, King Bhumibol summoned both Suchinda and Chamlong for a rare public scolding. Suchinda resigned, having been in power for less than six weeks, and Chamlong's career was at an end.

As the 20th century roared across Asia, fuelled by a burst of prosperity and creativity Thailand had never seen before, Bangkok grew from a mere 13 sq km (5 sq miles) in 1900 to an astounding metropolitan area of over 330 sq km (127 sq miles) by the century's end. However, in 1997 the Thai currency fell into a deflationary tailspin and the national economy screeched to a virtual halt. Bangkok, which rode at the forefront of the 1980s double-digit economic boom, was more adversely affected than elsewhere in the country by job losses and massive income erosion.

Struggling Democracy

In January 2001 after a landslide election victory, billionaire and former police colonel Thaksin Shinawatra was elected prime minister at the helm of a new party, Thai Rak Thai (TRT; Thai Love Thai). Thaksin's main support was among Thailand's rural poor because he proposed increased funding for health care and education. However, in the cities many quickly became disillusioned by the new government's authoritarianism and corruption.

In 2004 avian influenza turned up in Thailand's bird population and entire neighbourhoods in Bangkok were quarantined, particularly near Chatuchak Weekend Market

Greater Bangkok

Today Krung Thep Mahanakhon embraces not only Bangkok proper, but also the former capital of Thonburi, across the Chao Phraya River to the west, along with the densely populated 'suburb' provinces of Samut Prakan to the east and Nonthaburi to the north.

People power has played a major role in recent Thai politics

in northern Bangkok, where live birds are sold. By mid-2004 the epidemic had cost the Thai economy 19 billion baht. Worse was to come on 26 December 2004, when a massive tsunami hit Thailand's southern beaches, killing some 8,000 people.

In 2006 time began to run out for Thaksin. In January he enraged millions of Thais by selling off his private telecom company Shin Corp to a Singapore firm without paying any tax. Media mogul Sondhi Limthongkul set up the People's Alliance for Democracy (PAD) to protest against the government. In the wake of a series of demonstrations, including one that drew at least 100,000 protestors, Thaksin dissolved the government and held new elections. However, opposition parties boycotted the polls and many Thais refused to vote. Finally, in September 2006 a military junta overthrew Thaksin's government while he was at a UN meeting in New York.

The military installed Surayud Chulanont, a retired general, as a temporary prime minister, drafted a new constitution, and banned Thaksin and the the TRT party from politics. However, the general elections held in December 2007 were won by the People Power Party (PPP), a reincarnation of TRT led by Samak Sundaravej.

The PAD renewed its demonstrations against the PPP government. These came to a head in November 2008 when the PAD laid siege to Government House and seized Don Muang and Suvarnabhumi Airports for a week, leaving thousands of holidaymakers stranded in Bangkok. Under extreme pressure, the Constitutional Court ruled that the PPP should be disbanded for fraud and corruption.

The Oxford-educated leader of the Democrat Party Abhisit Vejjajiva formed a new coalition and became prime minister on 15 December 2008. He had long campaigned for cleaner and politics in Thailand, but his mandate is undermined by the fact that he was not democratically elected. Pro-Thaksin protestors have since caused chaos in the country, blocking roads in the capital and forcing the cancellation of an ASEAN summit in April 2009.

Today, the situation remains fragile. The long-term political and economical consequences of the crisis are still unclear. Bangkok groans under the weight of an overburdened infrastructure. Roads remain insufficient for the number of cars and up to 1,000 new vehicles climb onto the streets every day. But visitors can avoid the chaotic streets by using the clean and efficient Skytrain system, which opened in 1999, as well as the new metro network.

Overburdened roads

Historical Landmarks

1548 Ayuthaya merchants establish Thonburi Si Mahasamut on the banks of the Chao Phraya near the present site of Bangkok.

1767 Burmese armies sack Ayuthaya, and many Siamese flee south.

1782 Phaya Taksin moves the royal capital to Bang Makok.

1809 Rama II makes the restoration of Siamese art and culture a priority.

1844 The *Bangkok Recorder*, the country's first newspaper, is published.

1909 In response to heavy Chinese immigration, Siam requires the adoption of Thai surnames for all citizens.

1910–25 Under King Rama VI, primary education becomes compulsory and the Gregorian solar calendar becomes Siam's official calendar.

1932 A group of Paris-educated university graduates launches a bloodless revolution, turning Siam into a constitutional monarchy.

1935 Rama VII abdicates the throne without naming a successor.

1938 The People's Party appoints Field Marshal Phibul Songkhram as the first prime minister; the country's name is changed to Thailand.

1941 Japanese troops occupy Bangkok with Phibul's cooperation.

1964–73 The US establishes several army bases in Thailand to combat Communist expansion in neighbouring Indochina.

1973 A civilian government, led by academic Kukrit Pramoj, is elected.

1976 After hundreds of protestors are killed in demonstrations at Thammasat University, the Thai military seizes control of the government.

1982 General Prem Tinsulanonda issues a general amnesty, which effectively ends the Thai Communist insurgency.

1992 Civilians regain control of the government again.

1997 A steep devaluation of Thai currency leads to an economic crash.

1999 The BTS Skytrain opens.

2001 The new Thai Rak Thai (TRT) party sweeps elections.

2006 Military coup unseats Thaksin and the TRT.

2007 TRT party banned, PPP win general elections.

2008 PPP forced out of government. Abhisit Vejjaviva of the Democrat Party becomes the new prime minister.

2009 Pro-Thaksin protests cause the cancellation of and ASEAN summit.

WHERE TO GO

Although the sprawling capital of over 10 million may at first seem daunting, virtually every part of the city is accessible by elevated rail, Metro subway, river and canal boat services or city bus. For any place not easily reached by public transport, taxis are a reasonably priced alternative. Most of the neighbourhoods described in this chapter can be toured on foot.

KO RATTANAKOSIN (ROYAL ISLAND)

Resting in a bend of the Chao Phraya River, Bangkok's oldest district contains some of the city's most historic architecture – Wat Phra Kaew, the Grand Palace, Wat Pho and Wat Mahathat, along with the National Museum and the prestigious Thammasat and Silpakorn universities. The river bank in this area is busy with piers and markets, worthwhile attractions in themselves. Despite its name, Ko Rattanakosin is not an island at all, though in the days when Bangkok was known as the 'Venice of the East', Banglamphu Canal and Ong Ang Canal – two lengthy adjoining canals to the east that run parallel to the river – were large enough that the area felt like an island.

Teardrop-shaped Ko Rattanakosin is bounded to the west by the Chao Phraya, to the north by Phra Pin Klao Road and to the east by Atsadang Road and Khlong Lot. The district is accessible by boat via two Chao Phraya river piers, Tha Chang and Tha Maharat, or by road via taxi and public bus.

Grand Palace and Wat Phra Kaew

Also known by the English name, Temple of the Emerald Buddha, and more formally as Wat Phra Si Ratana Satsadaram,

Visiting the *stupas* at Wat Phra Kaew

the royal monastery of **Wat Phra Kaew** (daily 8.30am–11.30am, 1–3pm, pavilions Mon–Fri only; charge, includes admission to Dusit Park, *see page 55*) adjoins the Grand Palace on common ground consecrated in 1782, the first year of Bangkok rule. The 95-hectare (234-acre) palace grounds encompass over 100 buildings that represent more than 200 years of royal history and architectural experimentation. Most of the architecture is Rattanakosin or Old Bangkok style.

Inside a large chapel heavy with gilded ornamentation, the 66cm (26in) **Emerald Buddha** (actually carved from nephrite, a type of jade), after which the *wat* is named, sits in a miniature glass-paned pavilion with an intricately carved, five-tiered roof, on a pedestal high above the heads of worshippers. The

The Travelling Buddha

Neither the origin nor the sculptor of the Emerald Buddha is known for certain, but it first appeared in 15th-century Chiang Rai chronicles. Legend says it was carved in India and brought to Siam by way of Ceylon, but stylistically it belongs to northern Thailand's Chiang Saen or Lanna period of the 13th to 14th century. In the 15th century, the Buddha is thought to have been sealed with plaster and gold leaf and placed in Chiang Rai's own Wat Phra Kaew. While being carried to a new home, after a storm had damaged the *stupa* (reliquary) containing it, the Buddha lost its covering in a fall. It then stayed in Lampang for 32 years until it was brought to Wat Chedi Luang in Chiang Mai.

Lao invaders took the Emerald Buddha from Chiang Mai in the mid-16th century. It was returned 200 years later to the then Thai capital of Thonburi by General Chakri, later crowned as Rama I. When Bangkok became the capital, he moved the Buddha there and had two royal robes made for it, one for the hot season and the other for the rainy season. Rama III added another robe for the cool season. Either the king or the crown prince changes the robe at the beginning of each season.

enigmatic aura of the jade figure is enhanced by the fact that it cannot be examined closely, nor can it be photographed. Its lofty perch emphasises the image's occult significance as the most important talisman of the Thai kingdom and legitimator of Thai sovereignty.

The other temple structures are equally colourful and include gleaming, gilded *stupas* (Buddhist reliquaries), polished orange-and-green tiled roofs, mosaic-encrusted

Wat Phra Kaew's ornate roof

pillars and rich marble pediments. Extensive murals depicting scenes from the *Ramakian* (the Thai version of the Indian *Ramayana* epic) line the cloisters along the inside walls of the compound. Originally painted during Rama I's reign (1782–1809), the murals have undergone several restorations, including a major one finished in time for the 1982 Bangkok/Chakri dynasty bicentennial. Divided into 178 sections, the murals illustrate the epic in its entirety.

The king's current residence is Chitlada Palace in the northern part of the city, but the **Grand Palace** (Phra Borom Maharatchawong) is still used by the monarchy for selected ceremonial occasions such as Coronation Day. Although the actual palace is closed to the public, the exteriors of the four buildings are worth a swift perusal.

The largest Grand Palace structure, the triple-winged **Chakri Mahaprasat** (literally 'Great Holy Hall of Chakri', but usually translated as 'Grand Palace Hall') was designed by British architects in 1882 and displays a unique blend of

Grand Palace guard

traditional Thai and Italian Renaissance architecture, resulting in a style Thais call 'European wearing a Thai classical dancer's headdress', as each of the three wings is roofed with a tiered and heavily ornamented spire. The centrally positioned and tallest of the spires contains the ashes of Chakri kings, while the flanking spires hold those of Chakri princes. Thai kings traditionally housed their huge harems in the Chakri Mahaprasat's innermost halls, under the guard of combat-trained female sentries.

French-inspired **Borombiman Hall** served as residence for Rama VI, and is still occasionally used to house visiting foreign dignitaries. Originally a hall of justice, **Amarindra Hall** to the west is used only for coronation ceremonies in the present day. Further west stands **Dusit Hall**, originally built for royal audiences but later used as a royal funerary hall.

Wat Pho (Wat Phra Chetuphon)

Wat Pho (formally known as Wat Phra Chetuphon; daily 8am–5pm; charge; www.watpho.com) is the oldest and largest Buddhist temple in Bangkok and has the longest reclining Buddha in Thailand. The temple site, just south of the palace complex, dates from the 16th century, but the monastery was completely rebuilt in 1781 in preparation for the founding of the new Thai capital the following year.

Chetuphon Road divides the complex into two sections, each enclosed by high whitewashed walls. Only the northern section is open to the public and contains the *wat*'s most famous feature, a huge, gilded reclining Buddha image representing the passing of the Buddha into *parinibbana* (nirvana after death). Measuring 46m (151ft) long and 15m (49ft) high, the figure is made of brick moulded with plaster and finished in shining gold leaf. Mother-of-pearl inlays on the feet display the 108 different auspicious characteristics of a Buddha.

Two smaller sanctuaries to the east of the reclining Buddha contain the beautiful Phra Jinnarat and Phra Jinachi images, both originally cast in Sukhothai in northern Thailand. Galleries linking these chapels with two other chapels are lined with visually striking rows of seated gilded Buddha images, numbering 394 in all.

Rama I's remains are interred in the base of the presiding Buddha image in the main *bot* (ordination hall). Affixed to the lower exterior wall of the *bot* are 152 bas-reliefs, carved in mar-

The Buddha's giant feet at Wat Pho

Wat Pho's *stupas*

ble and obtained from the ruins of Ayuthaya, depicting scenes from the *Ramakian*. Temple rubbings offered for sale at Wat Pho come from cement casts of these panels.

Other notable structures in the northern compound include four large *stupas* commemorating the first three Chakri kings (Rama III has two *stupas*), 91 smaller *stupas*, an old Tipitaka (Buddhist scripture) library, a sermon hall, a school of Abhidhamma (Buddhist philosophy) and a traditional massage centre.

Wat Pho serves as the national headquarters for the teaching and preservation of traditional Thai medicine, including Thai massage, which is offered to temple visitors for a fee (tel: 0 2622 3533).

Lak Meuang and Sanam Luang

Bangkok's spiritual centre – and Km 0 for all mapping – is the **Lak Meuang** (City Pillar; daily 6am–6pm), standing across the street from the eastern wall of Wat Phra Kaew. The two-room, crowned pavilion shelters a 3m (9ft), gilded wooden pillar erected in 1782 during the founding of the new capital to worship the city's guardian deity, **Phra Sayam Thewathirat**. During the reign of Rama V, five smaller pillar idols were added to the shrine. The atmosphere of spirit worship is intoxicating, as Bangkokians stream in bearing pig heads and bottles of whisky to offer the spirit, while the shrine musicians hammer away on their wooden xylophones and brass gongs.

Sanam Luang (Royal Field), just north of Wat Phra Kaew, is the traditional site for royal cremations and for the annual Ploughing Ceremony, in which the king or the crown prince officially initiates the rice-growing season. The most recent ceremonial cremation took place here in March 1996, when the king presided over funeral rites for the queen mother.

Before 1982, when it was moved to Chatuchak Park in northern Bangkok, the city's famous Weekend Market *(see page 81)* convened weekly at Sanam Luang. Nowadays, the large field is used as a picnic and recreational area. A large kite-flying competition is held here during the kite-flying season (Mar–Apr). A **Mae Thorani statue**, representing Dharani (the Hindu-Buddhist earth goddess), occupies a white pavilion at the north end of the field. The 19th-century sculpture marks the site of a former public drinking well.

Wat Mahathat

Opposite Wat Phra Kaew, on the west side of Sanam Luang (Royal Field), **Wat Mahathat** (daily 7am–6pm) stands

Buddhist Insight Meditation

The monks at Wat Mahathat practise *satipatthana vipassana* (insight meditation) in the Dhamma Vicaya Hall on most days between 4am and 2pm (call ahead – tel: 0 2222 6011 – to make sure that an English-speaking instructor will be present). Meditation of this kind involves the noting of mental and physical sensations as they arise spontaneously until *vipassana* or insight into the essential nature of reality is acquired. Intensive, long-term residential instruction is also available at the monastery's International Buddhist Meditation Centre (tel: 0 2823 6326; www.mcu.ac.th/IBMC).

close to the Tha Maharat river pier. This large monastery was founded in the 18th century to serve as the national centre for the Mahanikai, the largest of Thailand's two monastic sects. It is also headquarters for Mahathat Ra-javidyalaya, one of Thailand's two Buddhist universities and the largest in Southeast Asia, with students from Laos, Vietnam and Cambodia.

While Wat Phra Kaew represents the capital's most elite temple, Wat Mahathat belongs very much to the masses and is all but neglected by foreign visitors. A daily open-air market features traditional Thai herbal medicine, and out on the street you'll find a string of shops selling herbal cures and offering Thai massage. At weekends, a large produce market held on the temple grounds brings hordes of people. Opposite the main entrance, on the other side of Maharat Road, lies a large Buddhist amulet market *(see page 83)*.

Wat Mahathat

Nearby **Silpakorn University** is partially housed in a former Rama I palace; Thailand's premier university for arts studies was originally founded as the School of Fine Arts by Italian artist Corrado Feroci (more commonly known by his royally bestowed Thai name, Silpa Bhirasri), who is considered Thailand's father of modern art. A small bookshop just inside the main gate stocks English-language books on Thai art.

Morning monks

Walk the streets of Bangkok early in the morning, and you'll catch the flash of shaved heads bobbing above bright ochre robes, as monks all over the city engage in *bindabaht*, the daily house-to-house gathering of alms food.

National Museum

At the northern end of Na Phra That Road, running along the west side of Sanam Luang, stands the **National Museum** (Wed–Sun 9am–4pm; charge), the largest museum in Southeast Asia and an excellent place to learn about Thai history, art and culture. All historical periods are represented, from Dvaravati (6th–10th century) to Rattanakosin (18th–early 20th century).

The stately buildings, originally built in 1782 as the palace of Rama I's viceroy, were turned into a museum in 1884. In addition to the exhibition halls, the museum grounds contain the restored **Buddhaisawan (Phutthaisawan) Chapel**. The 1795 chapel contains well-preserved original murals and one of the country's most revered Buddha images, the Phra

Buddhaisawan Chapel

Phuttha Sihing (which is said to come from Ceylon, although the stylistics indicate a 13th-century Sukhothai provenance). One of the more impressive rooms contains a well-maintained collection of traditional musical instruments from Thailand, Laos, Cambodia and Indonesia. Other permanent exhibits include ceramics, clothing and textiles, woodcarving, royal regalia, Chinese art and weaponry.

National Museum volunteers offer excellent free English-language tours of the museum on Wednesday (Buddhism) and Thursday (Thai art, religion and culture), starting from the ticket pavilion at 9.30am. Tours are also conducted in German (Thursday), French (Wednesday and Thursday) and Japanese (Wednesday).

Just to the south of the museum, **Thammasat University**, founded in 1934, is the country's most prestigious centre of higher learning for law and political science. The faculty and student body have also long been known for their political activism, and the campus was the site of bloody demonstrations against the Thai military dictatorship of Field Marshal Thanom Kittichorn in October 1976, during which hundreds of Thai students were killed or wounded by right-wing paramilitary groups. A plaque commemorating the incident stands on the field where the violence took place.

CHINATOWN AND AROUND

Bangkok's oldest residential and business district fans out along the Chao Phraya River between Phra Pin Klao Bridge and Hualamphong Railway Station. Largely inhabited by the descendants of Chinese residents who moved out of Ko Rattanakosin to make way for royal temples and palaces in the early 19th century, the neighbourhood is referred to by Thais as Sampeng (after the longest market lane, Soi Sampeng), or as Yaowarat (after the major avenue bisecting the district). The adjacent Indian market district, Phahurat, can be conveniently visited at the same time. Bangkok's busy Chinese and Indian market districts are best explored on foot, as vehicular traffic in the area is rather congested.

Chinatown, off Yaowarat and Ratchawong roads not far from the river, comprises a confusing and crowded array of jewellery, hardware, wholesale food, automotive and fabric shops, as well as dozens of other small businesses. Always effervescent, Chinatown fairly boils over with activity during the annual Vegetarian Festival, when Chinese Thais celebrate

Talat Kao market

Wat Mangkon Kamalawat

the first nine days of the ninth lunar month (September or October) with a culinary orgy of Thai and Chinese vegetarian fare. Bright yellow pennants flutter in front of noodle stalls, cafés and other eateries to signify that for those nine days, all food served in those establishments will be vegetarian.

The largest and liveliest temple in Chinatown, **Wat Mangkon Kamalawat** (Dragon Lotus Temple), faces onto Charoen Krung Road among shop-houses selling fruit, cakes, incense and ritual burning paper for offerings at the temple. Chinese and Tibetan inscriptions at the entrance give a brief history of the temple, while the labyrinthine interior features a succession of Mahayana Buddhist, Taoist and Confucian altars. Virtually day and night, this temple is packed with worshippers lighting incense, filling the ever-burning altar lamps with oil and praying to their ancestors.

Across Charoen Krung Road from the temple, Itsaranuphap Alley pierces deep into Chinatown's main market area. This section is flanked with vendors selling ready-to-eat and preserved foodstuffs, including cleaned fish and poultry. Though not for the squeamish, it's one of the cleanest fresh markets in Bangkok.

Down the lane looms the Chinese-lantern-hung entrance to **Talat Kao** (Talat Leng Buay La), a market that's been in continuous operation for over two centuries. All manner and size of freshwater and saltwater fish and shellfish are displayed here, alive and filleted. Continuing down towards the river, Itsaranuphap Alley crosses famous **Sampeng Lane** (Soi Wanit 1), the most crowded of Chinatown's market lanes, a gridlock of pedestrians, pushcarts and the occasional motorbike twisting through the crowds. Shops along this section of Sampeng Lane sell dry goods, especially shoes, clothing, fabric, toys and kitchenware.

Gold shops line **Yaowarat Road**, Chinatown's main thoroughfare, and for price and selection, this is probably the best place in Thailand to purchase a gold chain (sold by the *baht,* a 15g unit of weight).

In the 1920s and 1930s, Thai and foreign architects blended European Art Deco with functionalist restraint to create Thai Art Deco. Fully realised examples of this form can be found along Chinatown's main streets, particularly Yaowarat Road. Vertical towers over the main doorways are often surmounted with whimsical Deco-style sculptures – the Eiffel Tower, a lion, an elephant, a Moorish dome.

Perched on the top of a commercial building in **Songwat Road**, near Tha Ratchawong, is a rusting model of a World War II vintage Japanese Zero warplane, undoubtedly placed there by the Japanese during their brief 1941 occupation of Bangkok; in style and proportion it fits the surrounding Thai Art Deco elements.

Phahurat

At the western edge of China-town, Sampeng Lane leads to **Chakraphet Road**, the beginning of Phahurat, a district dominated by Indian-owned fabric shops. Chakra-

Thai Art Deco

Surviving examples of Thai Art Deco include the Chalermkrung Royal Theatre, the Royal Hotel, Ratchadamnoen Boxing Stadium and the General Post Office.

Phahurat Market

phet Road itself is well known for its Indian restaurants and shops selling Indian sweets. In a back alley on the west side of the road stands **Sri Gurusingh Sabha**, a large Sikh temple. Open to visitors, it claims to be the second-largest Sikh temple outside of India. Behind the temple, and stretching westward to Triphet Road, **Phahurat Market** is devoted almost exclusively to textiles and clothing.

Eastern Chinatown and Hualamphong

At the eastern edge of Chinatown near the intersection of Yaowarat and Charoen Krung roads, close to Hualamphong Railway Station, **Wat Traimit** (Temple of the Golden Buddha; daily 9am–5pm; charge) contains an impressive 3m (10ft) high seated Buddha image cast in solid gold. Moulded in the graceful Sukhothai style and weighing 5.5 tonnes, the image was 'rediscovered' some 40 years ago beneath a plaster exterior when it toppled from a crane while being transported to a new building in the compound. The covering may have been added to protect it from invading armies either during the Sukhothai or Ayuthaya periods. Although the temple site here may date from the early 13th century, Wat Traimit certainly took its current form no more than 200 years ago. To avoid the crowds, arrive in the early morning for a more traditional feel.

Bangkok's **Hualamphong Railway Station**, built by Dutch architects and engineers just before World War I, represents one of the city's earliest and most outstanding examples of Thai Art Deco. The vaulted iron roof and neo-classical portico demonstrate state-of-the-art engineering for the time, while the patterned, two-toned skylights exemplify De Stijl Dutch modernism.

Towards the southeastern edge of Chinatown, where Padung Krung Kasem Canal feeds back into the Chao Phraya River, a 19th-century Chinese entrepreneur named Chao Sua Son built a small market where larger riverboats could offload wholesale goods to Chinatown merchants. Walk down the main lane parallel to the canal and you'll come to **Chao Sua Son's home**, standing near the centre of the area now known as **Talat Noi** (Little Market). With a big round doorway opening onto a central courtyard surrounded by a U-shaped, one-storey building (now used as a company warehouse), it's one of very few surviving examples of traditional Chinese residential architecture in Thailand.

Wat Traimit's Golden Buddha

Under King Rama IV, the palace treasury found it could no longer cope with the complexities of burgeoning international trade, so the king granted a licence to Prince Mahissara Ratcha-haruthai to establish the Book (as in 'bookkeeping') Club in Talat Noi. The name was later changed to **Siam Commercial Bank**, today one of Thailand's three top banks. The early 20th-century, Rattanakosin-era bank still functions in its way, its tellers seated behind old-fashioned iron-grill windows, with the bank vault lying beneath the original tiled floor.

Talat Noi serves as a cultural and geographic bridge between the almost exclusively Chinese ambience of Yaowarat Chinatown to the north and the almost exclusively Western district – historically speaking, if not in present-day Bangkok – of European trading houses and embassies to the immediate south.

A portion of Talat Noi was given over to Portuguese residents, who in 1787 built the **Holy Rosary Church**, the cap-

ital's oldest place of Christian worship. Originally assembled of wood, after an 1890 fire it was replaced with brick and stucco in the neo-Gothic stucco style. Known in Thai as Wat Kalawan, from the Portuguese 'Calvario' (Calvary), the church features a Romanesque single-tower façade with a statue of the Virgin Mary surmounting the grand arched entrance. The interior is graced by Romanesque stained-glass windows, gilded ceilings and a very old, life-sized Jesus effigy, which is carried in the streets during Easter processions.

South of Talat Noi lies the commercial district of Bangrak (*see pages 66–8 for details*).

THONBURI

In the mid-16th century, during the height of Ayuthaya's power, forward-looking Thai merchants transformed the wooded western bank of the Chao Phraya River into an important trade entrepôt called Thonburi Si Mahasamut. When Ayuthaya fell to the Burmese in 1767, Siamese troops and the royal court shifted to Thonburi, which served as the capital of the Siamese kingdom for a brief 15 years.

Although today Thonburi comprises nearly half of metropolitan Bangkok in size and population, in many ways it happily lags behind the more modern cityscape on the opposite bank.

Longtail boats

Thonburi Canals

A vast network of **canals** criss-cross Thonburi in multiple directions, moving cargo and passengers, and providing a seemingly endless source of water for bathing, cooking, irrigation and recreation. Crowded water taxis weave among 'longtail' boats (named after the 3m/10ft propeller shafts jutting from the stern), ancient teak ferries and huge iron barges heaped with gravel or rice and chained together.

A longtail trip west off the Chao Phraya into **Bangkok Noi Canal** to the north seems to knock 50 years off big city progress, as the scenery transforms from high-rises into a snug corridor of teak houses on stilts, old Buddhist temples and banana groves. Thai women in straw lampshade-shaped hats hawk steaming bowls of rice noodles from wooden canoes. Mobile banks and post offices putter along atop tiny barges, further demonstrating that virtually any errand one might accomplish on land can also be done on water.

Royal Barges National Museum

Bangkok Noi Canal links up with Bang Yai Canal, site of **Wat Intharam**, where a *stupa* enshrines the ashes of Phaya Taksin. Fine *lai kham* (gold-and-black lacquerwork) adorning the chapel doors depicts a mythical tree which bears fruit in the shape of beautiful maidens.

From Bangkok Noi Canal, you can continue by boat up **Om Canal**, lined by plantations growing the spiky, strong-smelling durian. Another turn in the maze links up with **Mon Canal**, and you whoosh past gold-spired temples, century-old wooden piers and hothouses filled with exotic orchids.

Royal Barges National Museum

Building the canals

Using thousands of Khmer prisoners of war, King Rama I augmented Bangkok's natural canal-and-river system with hundreds of artificial waterways. All fed into Thailand's hydraulic lifeline, the broad Chao Phraya River, which bisected the city centre into two halves, Bangkok proper and Thonburi, the river's 'right bank'.

The Thai custom of royal boat processions dates to at least the reign of King Prasat Thong (1630–55) in the late Ayuthaya period, and Thailand's current royal dynasty has maintained the current fleet of majestic river vessels for nearly a century. The long, fantastically ornamented boats are still employed for ceremonial processions on the river. When not in use the watercraft are kept on public display in sheds that are part of the **Royal Barges National Museum** (9am–5pm; charge) on Bangkok Noi Canal, near its junction with the Chao Phraya River, not far from Phra Pin Klao Bridge.

Suphannahong, the King's personal barge, measures 50m (164ft) in length and is carved from a single piece of timber, making it the largest dugout in the world. The name means 'golden swan', and navigation requires a rowing crew of 50 men, plus seven umbrella-bearers, two helmsmen, two navigators, as well as a flagman, rhythm-keeper and chanter. A huge swan head has been carved into the bow and gilded. Lesser royal barges on display feature bows carved into *naga* (sea dragon) and *garuda* (Vishnu's bird mount) shapes.

Every year during the royal *kathin* (when new robes are offered to Buddhist monks) at the end of the annual Rains Retreat, the barges take to the river in a grand procession.

Forensic Medicine Museum

On the ground floor of the Forensic Medicine Building at Siriraj Hospital (on Phrannok Road, near Bangkok Noi Railway Station), the **Forensic Medicine Museum** (Mon–Sat 9am–4pm; charge) is the most famous of the 10 medical museums on the hospital premises. Grisly displays include the preserved bodies of some of the most famous Thai murderers (including Si Ouey, Thailand's equivalent of Jack the Ripper), clever murder weapons and other crime-related memorabilia.

Bangkok's Waterworld

Portuguese priest Fernão Mendez Pinto was the first to use the epithet 'Venice of the East', referring not to Bangkok but to Ayuthaya, in a letter to the Society of Jesus in Lisbon in 1554. Three hundred years later it came to be used to describe the new Bangkok capital as well, as in 1855, British envoy Sir John Bowring noted: 'The highways of Bangkok are not streets or roads but the river and the canals. Boats are the universal means of conveyance and communication.'

On the eve of the coronation of Rama VI in 1911, a young and adventurous Italian nobleman named Salvatore Besso wrote:

'The Venice of the Far East – the capital still wrapped in mystery, in spite of the thousand efforts of modernism amid its maze of canals… [T]he crowded dock-roads of the River… which reminds one of the Giudecca… the canals ploughed by sampans, which the rowers guide standing as in Venice… little bridges and tiny gardens, reflecting in the quiet water the drooping foliage of ancient trees… as in the remotest corners of the City of the Doges…'

Wat Arun at sunset

Wat Arun

The striking **Wat Arun**, or Temple of Dawn (daily 8am–6pm; charge), named after Aruna, the Indian god of dawn, features the tallest *stupa* in Bangkok and is probably the most photographed monument in the city after Wat Phra Kaew. An older monastery, 17th-century Wat Jang, once shared this site with Phaya Taksin's royal palace when Thonburi was the Thai capital, harbouring the Emerald Buddha before Rama I moved it across the river to Bangkok.

The 82m (270ft) *stupa*, constructed during the first half of the 19th century during the reigns of Rama II and Rama III, represents a unique design that elongates the typical Khmer 'corn cob' *stupa* tower into a distinctly more slender, Thai shape. The plaster covering the *stupa*'s brick core is embedded with a mosaic of broken, multi-hued Chinese porcelain, a common temple ornamentation in the early Rattanakosin period, when Chinese ships calling at Bangkok used tonnes of old porcelain as ballast. Steep stairs reach a lookout point about halfway up with fine views of Thonburi and the river.

Inside the ordination hall sits a large Buddha image said to have been designed by Rama II, whose ashes are contained in the base of the image. The walls are richly painted with Buddhist murals dating from Rama V's reign.

The grassy monastery grounds near the river make a peaceful retreat, and at night hundreds of lights illuminate the outline of the *stupa*, making it visible from a wide radius.

Santa Cruz Church

Portuguese Catholic missionaries were among the first Europeans to reside in Siam, first in Ayuthaya and later Bangkok. In 1770, they accepted a land grant in Thonburi from Phaya Taksin and built a simple wooden church known in Thai as **Kuti Jeen** (Chinese Cloister, since most of the congregation were Chinese converts). As the Portuguese presence diminished, the church gradually fell into disrepair until it was renovated in 1835 and renamed **Santa Cruz Church** (open Sat–Sun only). In 1913 the wooden church was demolished and re-

Santa Cruz Church

placed with a larger and more solid brick edifice that remains in use today, trimmed in maroon and cream, with a domed belfry and stained-glass windows. A spacious courtyard contains a tidy garden, a statue of the Virgin Mary and a large crucifix. The associated **Santa Cruz Convent School** is considered one of the capital's better non-government schools.

OLD BANGKOK

While Ko Rattanakosin was almost exclusively reserved for Thai nobility, areas to the east and north of Ko Rattanakosin were originally occupied by important government departments, commercial enterprises with royal connections and high-ranking monasteries. **Old Bangkok** (Banglamphu) still retains much of that character in parts, while a newer bohemian culture has filled other areas – Khao San Road, for example – where local commercial properties have been sold or rented.

Wall mural at Wat Suthat

Wat Suthat

Begun by Rama I and completed by Rama II and Rama III, **Wat Suthat** (daily 8.30am–9pm; charge) has a chapel containing several impressive gilded Buddha images, including Phra Si Sakayamuni, Thailand's largest Sukhothai-period bronze, along with jewel-toned murals chronicling tales from the Buddha's life. The main sanctuary is fitted with large wooden doors carved by various artisans of the period, including King Rama II himself. The ashes of Rama VIII (Ananda Mahidol, the current king's deceased older brother) are enshrined in the base of the presiding Buddha image.

Close to Wat Suthat stand two Brahmanist shrines, the **Thewa Sathan** (Deva Sthan) across the street to the northwest and the smaller **San Chao Phitsanu** (Vishnu Shrine) to the east. The former contains images of Shiva and Ganesha, while the latter is dedicated to Vishnu. These shrines hold a special place in the Thai spirituality because of their resident Brahman priests. The white-robed, Thai-Indian celibates perform important annual ceremonies, such as the Royal Ploughing Ceremony in May, on behalf of the entire nation.

Close to Wat Suthat, **Sao Ching-Cha** (Great Swing) was once the site of an astonishing Brahman festival in honour of the Hindu God Shiva each year. Participants would swing high above the ground in ever-higher arcs while trying to grab a bag of gold suspended from a 15m (50ft) bamboo pole. Many died trying, and during the reign of Rama VII (1925–35) the custom was halted.

Monk's Bowl Village (Ban Baht)

During the reign of the first Chakri monarch, Rama I (1782–1809), Siam's new royal capital dedicated three villages in Bangkok to the making of alms bowls for use by Buddhist monks to gather food from laypeople during their morning alms rounds. Today only one, **Ban Baht** (Monk's Bowl Village), survives, along a single narrow alley.

The average bowl-smith can only make one bowl a day, hammering out eight strips of metal in the traditional manner, fusing them in a wood fire with pellets of copper, then polishing the bowl and coating it with multiple layers of black lacquer. Only about half a dozen families still make the traditional alms bowls, and most of them are sold to wealthy Thais or tourists, as they are much more expensive than modern factory-made ones.

To find the village, walk south on Boriphat Road, south of Bamrung Meuang Road, then left on Soi Ban Baht. As you go along, you can browse the long rows of shops selling monks' robes and alms bowls.

The Golden Mount

Wat Saket is an undistinguished Rattanakosin-style temple famous only because of the **Golden Mount** (Phu Khao Thong; daily 7.30am–5.30pm; charge for the summit) in the western portion of the compound. A century ago it would have been the highest point in the city, offering unparalleled views of the city below, and still today, because of the lack of any high-rise buildings in the immediate vicinity, it's worth a climb for views of the local rooftops.

This hill was never natural and in fact was originally intended to be a large *stupa*. Construction began under Rama III (1824–51), but when the base collapsed because the soft soil couldn't support it, the brick *stupa* was abandoned. Rama IV (1851–68) later constructed a much smaller one atop the weed-choked mound of ruins. When the British government gave Thailand a Buddha relic from India, Rama V (1868–

Climbing the Golden Mount

1910) renovated the *stupa* to house the holy object, bringing the Golden Mount to its current height of 76m (250ft). To prevent erosion, concrete walls were added in the 1940s.

Wat Saket hosts one of Bangkok's largest temple festivals each November or December (depending on lunar phase) to honour the Buddha relic in the Golden Mount *stupa*. A candlelit procession up the hills marks the festival's high point.

The 7km (4-mile) long Banglamphu Canal curves gently inland from the river towards another wall-and-bunker cluster, **Mahakan Fort** (8.30am–6pm; free), marking the eastern edge of Old Bangkok. Of the 4m (13ft) high, 3m (10ft) thick ramparts that once lined the entire canal, only Phra Sumen *(see page 53)* and Mahakan have been preserved to remind us what 18th-century Bangkok really was about – keeping foreign armies at bay. Nearby is a small green park overlooking Ong Ang Canal.

Old fortifications

Open trade with the Portuguese, Dutch, English, French and Chinese had made Bangkok's fortifications obsolete by the mid-19th century, and most of the city's original wall was demolished to make way for sealed roadways.

Democracy Monument

In 1939 the Thai government decided that Bangkok needed a national monument commemorating the 1932 revolution that replaced Thailand's absolute monarchy with a constitutional one. The prime minister Phibul Songkhram chose a spot in the middle of Ratchadamnoen Road – originally designed for royal motorcades – as the site for the **Democracy Monument**. Feroci and his students from Bangkok's School of Fine Arts (SOFA) enclosed 75 cannonballs in the base of the monument to encode the year of the coup, BE 2475 (AD 1932). The main body of the monument consists of four Art Deco flanges that symbolise the cooperation of the army, air force, navy and police in the coup. Their 24m (79ft) height signifies the date of the coup, 24 June. Bas-relief scenes at the base depict the original coup leaders, the Thai people, the armed forces and a bucolic scene portraying 'Balance

Democracy Monument

and Good Life'. The flanges stand sentry around a bullet-shaped turret that enshrines a bronze casting of the 1932 constitution.

October 14 Memorial and Museum

This amphitheatre and museum commemorate the tragic events of 14 October 1973, when the Thai military fired upon a 500,000-strong crowd of pro-democracy protestors at the Democracy Monument, killing over 70. The demonstrators were protesting against the arrest of 13 students who had demanded a democratic constitution from Field Marshal Thanom Kittikachorn. Public revulsion at the massacre led to free elections in January 1975. The centrepiece of the memorial is a contemporary, secular interpretation of a Buddhist *stupa* made from granite blocks, built on the site of the former Thai TV News Agency, which had burned to the ground during the demonstrations. The walls of the adjacent elevated amphitheatre are decorated with historic pro-democracy posters and photographs taken on that fateful day. A spiral staircase leads underground to a library and **museum** displaying such historical memorabilia as the 16mm camera which student Shin Khlai-Pan used to record some of the 14 October 1973 events and the famous beret worn by protest organiser Seksan Prasertkul as he led the crowd down Ratchadamnoen Avenue.

Khao San Road

Well-to-do farmers and merchants from Ayuthaya who followed the royal court to Bangkok in the late 18th century

Arriving on the hectic Khao San Road

settled in Banglamphu – in the northern part of Old Bangkok – a reference to the lamphu tree *(Duabanga grandiflora)* once common to the area. By the time of Rama IV (1851–68), Banglamphu had become a flourishing commercial district, and **Khao San Road** was lined with two-storey shop-houses with a few teak mansions mixed in. By the early 1980s, two Chinese-Thai hotels on the road had been discovered by the European, American and Australian backpackers, and within a decade there were close to 100 guesthouses in the immediate vicinity (and today there are hundreds more).

Most of the two-storey shop-houses have been replaced by budget hotels, music and souvenir shops, restaurants, internet cafés, tattoo parlours and a myriad other services orientated towards the young and peripatetic. At night the street is closed off to vehicular traffic and a circus-cum-market atmosphere prevails, with vendors selling everything from colourful neo-hippie garb to *phat thai* (Thai-style fried noodles).

Phra Sumen Fort and Santichaiprakan Park

Standing on the banks of the Chao Phraya River in Banglamphu, off Phra Athit Road, **Phra Sumen Fort** (daily 5am–10pm) is named after Buddhist mythology's Mount Sumeru. The octagonal brick-and-stucco city fort was erected in 1783 as a defence against naval invasion and is one of only two remaining of the original 14 forts dotted along the Banglamphu Canal.

The grassy **Santichaiprakan Park** next to the bunker is a favourite spot for locals to picnic and enjoy river breezes. A broad, cement walkway follows the river south from the park to Phra Pin Klao Bridge. A stroll along it takes you past a handful of impressive residences built by Bangkok aristocrats in the late 19th and early 20th centuries. Today, most have been converted into headquarters for the Buddhist Society of Thailand, UNESCO and other non-profit organisations.

DUSIT

Dusit, an area centred around the royal palaces, associated outbuildings and extensive gardens, was inspired by Rama V's 1897 tour of Europe, particularly France and England. Upon his return the king and his courtiers decided that the former Grand Palace by the river was too cramped and old-fashioned, so they set about transforming an area of fruit orchards, extending Padung Krung Kasem and Samsen canals into an ambitious royal esplanade. Construction on Suan Dusit (Dusit Park) and the new palace began in 1900, and

Rama V Cult

The veneration of Rama V (aka King Chulalongkorn, 1868–1910) dates back to the 1991 military coup and the 1990–2 economic recession, when many Thais became disillusioned with politics and began looking for a new spiritual outlet with historical relevancy. The middle classes seized on Rama V, who, without the help of a parliament or the military, had brought Thai nationalism to the fore while fending off European colonisation. He is also revered for his abolition of slavery.

In Bangkok, the most visible devotional activities are focused on the bronze statue of Rama V in Royal Plaza, which has been transformed into a religious shrine. Every Tuesday, from 9pm until early in the morning, thousands of Bangkokians come to offer candles, flowers, incense and bottles of whisky to the newly ordained demigod.

Ironically, few Rama V devotees realise that the king conceded substantial Thai territory to French Indochina and British Malaya during his reign. Rama V also deserves more credit for the nation's Westernisation than any other monarch, being the first king to travel to Europe (in 1897 and 1907). After seeing Europeans eating with forks, knives and spoons, he discouraged the Thai tradition of taking food with the hands. He also introduced the use of chairs.

when completed in 1915 the complex encompassed three throne halls and 13 royal residences set among landscaped grounds covering 76 hectares (188 acres).

After the 1932 revolution ended absolute monarchy, and as 20th-century Bangkok began modernising, the crown relinquished much of the original palace grounds to commercial development in the area. The present Suan Dusit is thus about half the size it was when originally

Ananda Samakhom Throne Hall

established, and many royal promenades are today lined with government offices, schools and residential blocks. Still the area carries an air of grandeur and respect for the monarchy, with less of the urban chaos common in other precincts.

Dusit Park

The main southern entrance into **Dusit Park** (daily 9.30am–4pm; charge, or free for Grand Palace ticket-holders), now open to the public as the current king resides at the newer Chitrlada Palace nearby, is marked by Royal Plaza, a large roundabout at the end of Ratchadamnoen Road.

In the centre of the roundabout stands a bronze equestrian **statue of Rama V**. Although originally placed here as a mere historical monument, over the last two decades the statue has become the object of a devotional cult with the belief that the king's spirit resides at this spot *(see box opposite)*.

Behind Royal Plaza, the **Ananda Samakhom Throne Hall** is an Italian revival masterpiece designed by Italian architects Annibale Rigotti and Mario Tamagno. The domed hall housed the Thai parliament after the 1932 revolution.

Beyond the throne hall lies the pièce de résistance of Dusit Park, **Vimanmek Mansion** (guided tours only lasting an hour; every half-hour 9.30am–3pm; available in several languages). Rama V originally built this beautiful Victorian mansion on the island of Ko Si Chang in 1868. Later, because the Gulf of Thailand was deemed vulnerable to French invasion, Vimanmek was moved to its present site in 1910. The extraordinary L-shaped, three-storey residence contains 81 rooms, halls and anterooms, along with dozens of grand staircases, and is said to be the world's largest golden teak building. Rooms display Rama V's personal effects as well as an impressive collection of early Rattanakosin art and antiques. The tours cover around 30 rooms. Traditional Thai classical and folk dances are performed at

Vimanmek Mansion is the world's largest golden teak building

10.30am and 2pm in a pavilion off the canal side of the mansion.

Nearby, **Abhisek Dusit Throne Hall** is a smaller wood and brick-and-stucco building, opened in 1904 to receive visiting dignitaries. Typical of the finer architecture of the era, the Victorian-influenced gingerbread and Moorish porticoes blend to create a striking and distinctly Thai exterior. The hall displays traditional Thai arts and crafts, sponsored by the Promotion of Supplementary Occupations and Related Techniques (SUPPORT), a royal foundation under the patronage of Queen Sirikit.

Abhisek Dusit Throne Hall's striking porticoes

Two elephant stables that once housed three 'white' elephants – animals whose relatively pale hide and auspicious markings meant they would be automatically offered to the king – have been converted into the **Royal Elephant Museum**. Exhibits of photos, tools and artefacts associated with Thai elephant lore are on display, as well as the ranking system for the royal elephants. In one of the stables stands a lifelike sculpture of one of the most important royal elephants (now kept at the Chitrlada Palace).

Two residence halls to the north of Vimanmek are now used to house the **HM King Bhumiphol Photography Exhibitions**, a collection of the king's photography, as well as photos of the king and the royal family.

Nearby, **Princess Orathai Thep Kanya Residential Hall** contains displays of rare and beautiful silk and cotton textiles

Mowing the grass in Dusit Park

that were woven during the reigns of Rama IV and Rama V.

Other palace-complex structures open to the public include the **Suan Kularb Residential Hall and Throne Hall**, once home to King Rama V's son Prince Atsdang Dejavudh. The two red-roofed buildings appear to blend Tudor, Victorian and Swiss chalet elements. Today, they're used to display the king's collection of paintings (some painted by His Majesty, some by other artists).

Near the north entrance to Dusit Park, the **Royal Carriage Museum** displays 13 royal horse carriages (for the king and queen) and palanquins (for courtiers) that were used by the court of Rama V in the pre-automobile era.

Suan Si Rue Di, a more traditional Thai residence raised on stilts and featuring exterior stairways and hipped roofs trimmed with Victorian details, once served as a residence for Queen Saovabha and Princess Valaya Alongkorn (aunt to the current king). The hall displays a collection of gifts that were presented to King Bhumibol on the 50th and 60th anniversaries of his coronation.

Tamnak Ho was built for Rama V's son Prince Paribatra Sukhumbandhu, but today houses a collection of 13th-century Sukhothai ceramics salvaged from Gulf of Thailand shipwrecks. This residence was moved from another part of the city to its present position in 1998.

Suan Bua, formerly a home for Princess Saisavali Bhiromya, one of Rama V's favourite consorts, displays a striking collection of Buddha images, historic photographs from the Rama VI era, and gifts presented to King Bhumibol by visiting heads of state.

Krom Luang Vorased Thasuda Residential Hall, once home to Rama III's daughter Princess Bootri, is used for an exhibit of ancient pottery from Ban Chiang, a civilisation that flourished in northeastern Thailand 4,000 to 8,000 years ago.

Dusit Zoo

Rama VIII gave his private botanical garden, Khao Din Wana, to the people of Bangkok in 1938 for the purpose of creating a zoological garden. Located between Chitrlada Palace and the National Assembly Hall, with the main entrance off Ratwithi Road, the 19-hectare (47-acre) **Dusit Zoo** (8am–6pm; charge) harbours over 1,600 species of mammals, reptiles and birds, including relatively rare indigenous species and one of the best collections of gibbons anywhere in the world.

Even for visitors not particularly interested in the animal kingdom, the zoo makes a pleasant retreat from city noise and dust. Plants and trees in the ample grounds are labelled in English, Thai and Latin, and an artificial lake in the centre offers paddleboats for rent. A small fun park with a playground and amusement park rides will help entertain small children. Lakeside restaurants serve inexpensive Thai food. Weekdays are much less crowded than weekends.

CENTRAL BANGKOK

A nexus of upscale hotels, plush shopping malls, state-of-the-art cinemas, foreign embassies, the National Stadium and Thailand's most prestigious university, central Bangkok is a magnet for both Thai residents and visiting foreigners.

Jim Thompson's House

Jim Thompson's House (Soi Kasem San 2, Rama I Road; daily 9am–5pm; charge; www.jimthompsonhouse.org), just north of the National Stadium Skytrain station, is the former residence of American silk entrepreneur Jim Thompson, who almost single-handedly popularised Thai silk worldwide.

Thompson, an architect by training, joined the Office of Strategic Services, which later became the CIA, during World War II and served in France and, after the war ended, in Ceylon and Thailand for a brief time. When he was discharged from the military, he took a commission to renovate the now famous Oriental Hotel, before founding his Thai Silk Company in 1947. The company began turning a profit in its very first year, as his renditions of traditional Thai silk colours and patterns – which at the time were in danger of disappearing – became popular in the Milan, London and Paris fashion worlds.

Thompson became an avid collector of Thai and Southeast Asian art, and was one of the first Westerners living in Thailand to become interested in traditional Thai teak homes. Collecting six derelict houses in central

Jim Thompson's House

Thailand, he reassembled them in 1959 to create one of the most envied residential compounds in Bangkok.

The silk king mysteriously disappeared in 1967, while walking on holiday in Malaysia's Cameron Highlands. Despite massive search efforts, no trace of him was ever found. The Thai government turned Thompson's sumptuous residence, complete with his collection of art and antiques, into a museum, including a gallery, silk showroom and café.

Inside Jim Thompson's House

Siam Square

To the southeast, on the other side of Phaya Thai Road, off Rama I Road, **Siam Square**, a grid of 12 short lanes *(see pages 84–6)*, is where Bangkok's cutting edge blends into trendiness, forged into Thai pop culture by television and the other mass media. At weekends in particular, Siam Square draws hordes of Thai teenagers who hang out in local cafés and noodle shops, perch in twos and threes on Siam Centre's massive steps or prowl the claustrophobic inter-lane alleyways for inexpensive local designer clothing.

On Saturday afternoons an outdoor section of Siam Square, informally known as Centrepoint, becomes an impromptu rendezvous for Thai youngsters showing off the results of their visits to Siam Square tattoo parlours and punk hair salons, accompanied by live music from an outdoor stage.

Wang Suan Pakkard

Prince Chumbhot of Nakhon Sawan and his wife Mom Ratchawong Pantip brought five 19th-century Thai houses down from Chiang Mai and reassembled them in 1952 to serve as their residence. The prince added a sixth teak structure from a monastery in Ayuthaya in 1958, and two contemporary buildings were built later to house the royal couple's extensive collection of art and artefacts. Known as **Wang Suan Pakkard** (daily 9am–4pm; charge), or Cabbage Farm Palace, the eight houses on the Ayuthaya Road are filled with historic Thai Buddha images, Ban Chiang ceramics, Khmer Hindu-Buddhist art and antique furnishings.

Gaysorn Plaza lobby

The Ayuthaya-style monastery chapel, popularly known as the **Lacquer Pavilion**, is famous for its sumptuous gold-leaf-on-lacquer murals illustrating episodes from the *Ramakian*, the life stories of the Buddha and scenes from daily Ayuthaya life.

Erawan Shrine

On the corner of Ratchaprarop and Ploenchit roads, next to the Grand Hyatt Erawan Hotel, stands the **Erawan Shrine**, originally built to ward off bad luck during the construction of the original Erawan Hotel (torn down to make way for the Grand Hyatt some years ago). The four-headed deity at the centre of the shrine is Brahma, the Hindu god of creation. At first a typical Thai spirit house was erected, but was replaced with the Brahma shrine after several mishaps delayed the hotel construction. Worshippers who have a wish granted may return to commission the musicians and dancers who are always ready to perform.

Thap Thim Shrine

Worshipping at Erawan Shrine

At the back of the Swissôtel Nai Lert Park on Withayu Road, the unusual **Thap Thim Shrine** consists of clusters of carved stone and wooden phalluses surrounding a spirit house built by Bangkok millionaire Nai Lert in homage to Chao Mae Thap Thim, a female spirit believed to inhabit a large banyan tree behind. According to legend, a woman who left an offering of a wooden phallus here asking to get pregnant had her wish granted. Word spread, other women seeking fertility began doing the same and the shrine is now overflowing with phalluses, in all shapes, sizes and colours.

Returning to the south of Siam Square, you will find **Chulalongkorn University**, founded in 1917 by Rama VI. The kingdom's oldest and most selective university occupies a huge tract of land extending between Rama I and Rama IV roads. Today it is famous for its arts and humanities, biomedicine and for the Sasin Graduate Institute of Business Administration, attended by students from all over Asia and beyond.

The older buildings on campus, a blend of Rattanakosin and Italian revival architecture, surround a grassy parade ground and a seated statue of Rama V (King Chulalongkorn), after whom the university was named. The cultural centre for student performing arts is home to the **Jamjuree Art Gallery**, which hosts changing exhibits of student artwork.

Snake Farm

Formerly known as the Pasteur Institute, and more commonly called Snake Farm, the Thai Red Cross-sponsored **Queen Saovabha Memorial Institute** (Phra Ram IV Road; Mon–Fri 8.30am–3.30pm, Sat–Sun 9.30am–1pm; charge), just south of the university, is a favourite stop for visitors keen to see the milking of Thailand's six venomous snake species – common cobra, king cobra, banded krait, Malayan pit viper, green pit viper and Russell's viper. Raised in captivity, the snakes are milked daily to produce snake-bite antidotes, which are distributed to clinics and hospitals

Enjoying the show at the Snake Farm

throughout Thailand. Founded in 1923, the institute became the second antivenin research facility in the world, after one in Brazil. Unlike other 'snake farms' in Bangkok, this is a serious herpetological research facility, named after Rama V's queen, a pioneer in promoting health education in Thailand.

The public **milking sessions** (weekdays 11am and 2.30pm, weekends and holidays 11am only) are a major Bangkok attraction. An informative half-hour slide show on snakes is presented before the milking sessions.

Lumphini Park

One road east of the Snake Farm, Bangkok's oldest public park, **Lumphini Park** (daily 5am–8pm) was established on crown land given to the city by Rama VI in 1925. At the time, Thailand was embroiled in an economic recession, and the king knew the building of the park would provide much-needed jobs. He also invited farmers and merchants to mount an exhibition of local products and natural resources for a year, and afterwards named the 14-hectare (35-acre) grounds Lumphini Park (the Thai pronunciation of Lumbini, the birthplace of the Buddha in Nepal).

Called 'Suan Lum' by locals, the park is bounded by Rama IV, Ratchadamri and Withayu roads. Interspersed among spacious grassy tracts stand the city's oldest public library (8am–8pm), a dance hall, a senior citizens' club, a youth centre, a tea shop and a weight lifting area. A statue of Rama VI stands at the southwestern entrance to the park. From mid-February until April, during the kite-flying season, the park is full of kites, which are also available to buy here.

Visit Suan Lum in the early morning to see local residents practising t'ai chi, drinking tea and herbal tonics or jogging along the network of pathways. On the other side of Withayu Road, opposite the park, **Suan Lum Night Bazaar** offers informal dining, shopping and live music nightly.

The intricately decorated Sri Mariamman Temple

SILOM/BANGRAK

In the 19th and early 20th centuries, when Bangkok's large sailing ships and steamships would navigate up the Chao Phraya River, the more prominent international trade firms and foreign embassies placed their headquarters on the banks of **Bangrak**, south of Ko Rattanakosin and Chinatown. Serving a primarily foreign clientele, the legendary Oriental Hotel began its career here as a humble riverside lodge in 1865; today it is one of the city's most luxurious temporary addresses.

Alongside European residents, migrants from India and Pakistan conducted their businesses in the gem and fabric trades, and still do so today in the many shops lining **Charoen Krung Road** (the first road in the capital to be sealed, in 1861), which follows the river for 10km (6 miles), linking Bangrak with Old Bangkok.

Heading inland from Charoen Krung, **Silom Road** was also built mainly to serve the Europeans and South Asians. Instead of trade and shipping concerns, businesses along here were focused on banking, finance and insurance. Later on, Silom Road (and parallel Surawong Road) became a popular location for airline offices and hotels, which led to the development of the famous red-light district of Patpong.

Close to where Silom and Charoen Krung roads meet stands the Cathedral of the Assumption of the Blessed Mary, or the **Assumption Cathedral**, as it's generally known. French missionaries became influential in Bangkok in the 19th century and built a Catholic church on this site, close to the river, in 1822. This was replaced by a larger Romanesque church between 1910 and 1918, which was badly damaged in World War II. The church was promoted to cathedral status in 1965, and in 1984 Pope John Paul II said Mass here. The cathedral is found on the same lane as the famous **Oriental Hotel**.

Sri Mariamman Temple (Maha Uma Devi Temple)

Called Wat Phra Si Maha Umathewi in Thai (or simply Wat Khaek, 'Indian Temple'), the **Sri Mariamman Temple** (daily 6am–8pm; free) sits at the intersection of Silom and Pan roads in Bangrak. Built in the mid-19th century by Tamil immigrants, this Hindu sanctuary features a colourful tower decorated with sculptures of Hindu deities in classical South Indian style. A gold-plated copper dome tops off the tower, and inside the small temple interior is a shrine altar dedicated to Uma Devi (Shiva's consort), flanked by shrines for her elephant-headed son Ganesha and her son Khanthakumara. For good measure, lesser walls are festooned with figures of Shiva, Vishnu and Buddha. Bright yellow marigold garlands are sold at the entrance for use as offerings.

Assumption Cathedral

An interesting ritual takes place in the temple at noon on most days, when a priest brings out a tray carrying an oil lamp, coloured powders and holy water. He sprinkles the water on the hands of worshippers, who in turn pass their hands through the lamp flame for purification; they then dip their fingers in the coloured powder and daub prayer marks on their foreheads. On Friday at around 11.30am, *prasada* (blessed vegetarian food) is offered to devotees.

Kukrit Pramoj Heritage House

Across the Sathorn Canal, the sprawling **Kukrit Pramoj Heritage House** at 19 Soi Phra Phinit (off Sathorn Tai Road; Sat–Sun 9.30am–5pm; charge) is the former residence of the prolific author and statesman M.R. Kukrit Pramoj (1911–95). Educated at Oxford, he was the great-grandson of Rama II and uncle to Rama IX (the current king), and served as Thailand's prime minister in 1974 and 1975. Five traditional Thai teak houses occupy the main section of the compound, and behind them is a large garden decorated with Khmer stone art.

Patpong

Back on the northern side of the Sathorn Canal, the district known as **Patpong**, notorious for its go-go bars and sex shows, lies along two pedestrian-only lanes between Silom and Surawong roads. Patpong got its start as a convenient entertainment spot for international staff working at nearby airline offices in the late 1950s and early 1960s, and was further boosted by the arrival of US and Australian soldiers during the early 1970s Indochina War era. Patpong has slowly tamed itself over the years (much less total nudity nowadays, for example) and has transformed from a male-only enclave to a more general tourist attraction. Although the neon-lit go-go action continues to this day, the **Patpong night bazaar** – rows of vendor carts hawking everything from cheap T-shirts to knock-off DVDs and fake designer watches in the middle of Patpong Soi 1 – has become an added draw.

Charter boats depart from Nonthaburi

EXCURSIONS FROM BANGKOK

When you've had enough of Bangkok's intensity, there are several spots outside the city you can escape to for a day or overnight. Within a 150km (93-mile) radius, you can choose among 16th- to 18th-century temple ruins in Ayuthaya, the tallest Buddhist monument in the world at Nakhon Pathom, the world-famous 'Bridge on the River Kwai' in Kanchanaburi and a park filled with scaled-down versions of historical architecture from all over the country. Closer is the river island of Ko Kret in Nonthaburi.

Ko Kret

An island in the middle of the Chao Phraya River in Nonthaburi, at Bangkok's northern edge, **Ko Kret** is home to one of Thailand's oldest Mon settlements. The Mon, who between the 6th and 10th centuries AD were the dominant culture in

Samut Prakan Crocodile Farm and Zoo

central Thailand, are skilled potters, and Ko Kret remains one of the oldest and largest sources of earthenware in the region. An exhibit of local pottery can be seen at the **Ancient Mon Pottery Centre**. You can also watch the locals crafting pottery.

Wat Porami Yikawat, known simply as Wat Mon, contains a Mon-style marble Buddha imported from Myanmar. Meditation retreats and courses are offered by **Baan Dvara Prateep** (www.baandvaraprateep.com) in a complex of wooden houses on stilts on the west of the island.

The easiest way to reach Ko Kret on Sundays is to catch the special Chao Phraya River Express boat from Tha Sathon direct to the island. It departs at 10am and returns at 4.30pm. At other times take the Chao Phraya River Express boat to Pak Kret Pier, then take a cross-river public ferry to Ko Kret.

Ancient City (Muang Boran)

Covering over 120 hectares (300 acres), **Ancient City** (Muang Boran; daily 8am–5pm; charge; www.ancientcity.com) claims to be the largest open-air museum in the world. The outline of the complex mimics Thailand's geographical shape and encompasses 116 facsimiles of the kingdom's most famous monuments, along with related ponds, canals, gardens and linking walkways, offering a quick archaeological tour of the country. Monuments run the gamut from the stately temple ruins of Sukhothai in the north to the venerated Phra Boromathat *stupa* in Nakhon Si Thammarat in the south. Some are full-scale replicas, while others have been scaled down to one-third or three-quarters of the original. Wear comfortable shoes, as it takes a whole day to cover the huge area.

Ancient City has plenty of open space for picnics and leisurely walks. Bicycles are available for rent for visitors who would rather pedal their way round the complex. Snacks are available from boat vendors on the canals.

In the same area, **Samut Prakan Crocodile Farm and Zoo** (daily 7am–6pm; charge) has over 30,000 crocodiles (including Yai, the largest croc in captivity at 1,115kg/2,450lbs), along with other animals. There are trained animal shows hourly, and feeding time is 4–5pm.

Ayuthaya

Wat Phra Si Sanphet

Thailand's royal capital from 1350 to 1767, the city of **Ayuthaya** is 86km (53 miles) north of Bangkok. It was named after Ayodhya (Sanskrit for 'unassailable' or 'undefeatable'), which is the home of Rama in the Indian epic *Ramayana*. City planners located the city at the confluence of the Chao Phraya, Pa Sak and Lopburi rivers, and added a wide canal to form a full circle of water around the town as a defence.

Ayuthaya's 400-year reign was Siam's historical apex, with sovereignty extending well into present-day Laos, Cambodia and Myanmar, and the kingdom's longest-enduring royal lineage (33 kings reigned before Ayuthaya was conquered by the Burmese in 1767). Thai culture and international commerce flourished, and the kingdom was courted by European, Chinese and Japanese merchants. By the end of the 17th century, Ayuthaya's population had reached 1 million – many foreign visitors recorded it to be the most illustrious city they had ever seen.

Today, Ayuthaya has preserved many of its Buddhist temple ruins, which together make up **Ayuthaya Historical Park**, a UNESCO World Heritage Site. Regular buses and trains to Ayuthaya leave Mo Chit bus terminal and Hualam-

Ayuthaya Festivals

Ayuthaya holds one of the country's largest Loi Krathong festivals at the full moon of the 12th lunar month, usually November. Celebrations are held at several spots in Ayuthaya, with the largest spectacle taking place at Beung Phra Ram, a large lake in the centre of the city between Wat Phra Ram and Wat Mahathat. Tens of thousands of people, many from Bangkok, flock to the Beung Phra Ram event to crowd around five outdoor stages hosting *likay* (bawdy folk plays with dancing and music), Thai pop, outdoor cinema and *lakhon chaatre*e (classical dance-drama). Food vendors and fireworks play a major part in the festivities. More low-key and traditional is the celebration at the Chan Kasem Pier, where families launch their *krathong* (small lotus-shaped floats made from banana leaves and topped with incense, flowers, coins and candles) onto the junction of the Lopburi and Pa Sak rivers. For a few baht you can be paddled out to the middle of the river to launch your own *krathong*.

Another major site for Loi Krathong is the Royal Folk Arts & Crafts Centre in Bang Sai, about 24km (15 miles) west of Ayuthaya. Here the emphasis is on traditional costumes and handmade *krathong*.

For 10 days before the Songkran Festival, the Thai New Year celebration in mid-April, a sound-and-light show is held in the temple ruins.

phong station in Bangkok, but the most pleasant way to get here is by boat – several agencies offer day trips.

Buddha head covered in banyan tree roots at Wat Mahathat

Although a modern city has encircled the ruin sites, Ayuthaya's historic temples are scattered throughout the island part of the city and along the encircling rivers and canal. Several of the more central ruins – **Wat Phra Si Sanphet**, **Wat Mongkhon Bophit**, **Wat Phra Ram**, **Wat Thammikarat**, **Wat Ratburana** and **Wat Mahathat** – can be visited on foot or rented bicycle. **Wat Phanan Choeng**, **Wat Phutthaisawan**, **Wat Kasatthirat** and **Wat Chai Wattanaram** are most conveniently toured by chartering a longtail boat.

Two museums, **Chao Sam Phraya National Museum** and **Chantharakasem National Museum** (both Wed–Sun 9am–4pm; free) contain exhibits of Thai Buddhist art and archaeology, with an emphasis on the Ayuthaya period. The newer **Ayuthaya Historical Study Centre** (Mon–Fri 9am–4.30pm, Sat–Sun 9am–5pm; charge) offers further insight into Ayuthaya's history with professionally curated displays focusing solely on the city.

Many visitors to Ayuthaya also visit **Bang Pa-In** (daily 8.30am–3.30pm; charge), a summer palace complex built by Rama IV (and used by his son Rama VI as well), 20km (12 miles) to the south. The most photographed feature of the complex is a pretty little Thai pavilion in a small lake by the entrance. Also of note are the Chinese-roofed **Wehat Cham-**

Phra Pathom Chedi

run **Palace** and **Withun Thatsana** tower, which offers a fine view over the lakes and gardens, including a topiary with bushes trimmed to resemble a small herd of elephants.

Across the river and south from the palace grounds, **Wat Niwet Thamaprawat** is a Buddhist temple built by Rama V in 1878 in the style of a Christian church, complete with stained-glass windows and Gothic spires.

Phra Pathom Chedi

Nakhon Pathom (population 50,000), 56km (35 miles) west of Bangkok, is often called the oldest city in Thailand, and its name in fact means 'First City'. It may once have served as the power centre for the Dvaravati kingdom, a collection of Mon city-states that flourished between the 6th and 11th centuries AD. The town's world-famous **Phra Pathom Chedi**, at 127m (417ft) the tallest Buddhist monument in the world, is said to encase a 6th-century *stupa* within its huge ochre-glazed dome.

In the early 11th century, Khmer king Suryavarman I conquered Nakhon Pathom and built an Angkor-style tower over the Mon *stupa*. In 1869, after Burmese armies sacked the city in 1057, the tower lay in ruins until Rama IV restored the monument in 1860, building the current larger *stupa* over the remains. A **national museum** (Wed–Sun 9am–4pm; charge) contains displays of Dvaravati-era sculpture and other artefacts.

Floating Markets

Several floating markets can be visited along canals to the southwest of Bangkok in Samut Songkhram and Ratchaburi provinces. **Ton Khem Floating Market**, a century-old market on Damnoen Saduak Canal around 100km (62 miles) southwest of Bangkok, is the largest, while **Hia Kui Floating Market**, just south of Damnoen Saduak on parallel Hia Kui Canal, is the most popular with visitors. A third, somewhat less crowded market can be found on nearby Khun Phitak Canal at **Khun Phitak Floating Market**. Boats can be rented to tour the canals and all three markets. Try to arrive by 8am at the latest, as by 9am the markets are very crowded.

Around 7km (4 miles) northwest of Samut Songkhram, **Amphawa Floating Market** (Fri–Sun 4–9pm) operates weekend evenings in front of Wat Amphawa – the perfect floating market for late risers.

Damnoen Saduak floating market

Kanchanaburi

Around 130km (80 miles) west of Bangkok, in the slightly elevated Mae Klong River valley, **Kanchanaburi** is surrounded by hills and sugar-cane plantations. Rama I originally established the town as a first line of defence against the Burmese who might invade via Three Pagodas Pass on the Thai-Burmese border.

During World War II, the Japanese built the infamous Death Railway along this same invasion route, in reverse, along the Khwae Noi River, using Allied prisoners of war and Southeast Asian draft labourers. Thousands died as a result of brutal treatment by their captors, a story chronicled by Pierre Boulle's *The Bridge on the River Kwai*, which was made into an Oscar-winning film of the same name (1957) by David Lean.

Death Railway Bridge

The steel **Death Railway Bridge** (the bridge on the River Kwai) still spans the Khwae Yai River, a tributary of the Mae Klong, 3km (nearly 2 miles) from the centre of town. The strategic objective of the railway was to secure an alternative supply route for the Japanese conquest of Burma (Myanmar) and other Asian countries to the west. The materials for the bridge were brought from Java by the Imperial Japanese Army during their occupation of

Thailand. The first version of the bridge, completed in February 1943, was all wood. In 1945, the bridge was bombed several times and was only rebuilt after the war – the curved portions of the bridge are original. An estimated 16,000 prisoners of war died while building the 415km (258-mile), narrow-gauge Death Railway to Burma, roughly two-thirds of which ran through Thailand. Death rates of labourers from Thailand, Burma, Malaysia and Indonesia were even higher: 90,000 to 100,000 in 16 months.

The deadly bridge

In normal times, a 415km (258-mile) rail line through difficult terrain would have taken five years to complete, but in World War II, the Japanese forced the POWs and coolies to complete it in 16 months. The Japanese used the infamous bridge for only 20 months before it was bombed by the Allies in 1945.

The best place to start your exploration of the Kanchanaburi area is at the **Thailand-Burma Railway Centre Museum** (daily 9am–5pm; charge), where you can walk through eight galleries of displays chronicling the history of the railway and Japanese aggression in Southeast Asia during World War II.

Opposite the museum, the **Kanchanaburi Allied War Cemetery** (also known as Don-Rak War Cemetery; daily 7am–6pm; free) contains the graves of 6,982 Australian, Dutch and British prisoners of war, who lost their lives during the construction of Death Railway. Lovingly tended, the cemetery is a touching gift from the Thai people to the countries whose citizens died on their soil. The less visited **Chung Kai Allied War Cemetery** commemorates more soldiers.

Best and most moving of all is the smaller **JEATH War Museum** (daily 8.30am–6pm; charge) occupies a portion of the grounds of Wat Chaichumphon and displays replicas of the bamboo huts used to shelter prisoners of war. Inside the the huts are war-era photos, drawings and paintings by the prisoners, weapons and other war memorabilia. JEATH stands for Japan, England, Australia/America, Thailand and Holland, the six countries who were embroiled at Kanchanaburi during World War II.

Kanchanaburi District is also famous for its cave temples. At **Wat Tham Mongkon Thong**, dragon-banister stairs ascend a steep slope to reach a complex of limestone caves filled with Buddha images and other sacred sculptures. Every Sunday a white-robed Thai Buddhist nun displays Buddha-like hand gestures while floating on her back in a round water tank, a devotional exhibition known to tour guides as the 'floating nun'. Devotees from all over Thailand come to watch the ritual and to receive the nun's blessings.

Two larger cave monasteries, Wat Tham Seua and Wat Tham Khao Noi, sprawl across a mountain ridge 15km (9 miles) southeast of Kanchanaburi. **Wat Tham Seua**'s dominating feature is a large seated Buddha overlooking the Mae Klong River. An alms bowl in the figure's lap receives money offerings sent to it via a hand-operated conveyor belt. Steps to the right of the monastery's main entry stairs lead up to an aviary harbouring a variety of tropical birdlife and to a cave that is filled with Buddhas.

The Chinese temple architecture of **Wat Tham Khao Noi** is inspired by Penang's Kek Lok Si. A stroll to the top of the complex yields some impressive views of the Khwae River and agricultural fields.

> ### Escape to Ko Samet
>
> Sunthon Phu's *Phra Aphaimani* follows the travails of a prince exiled to an undersea kingdom ruled by a lovesick female giant. A mermaid aids the prince in his escape to Ko Samet, where he defeats the giant by playing a magic flute.

Ko Samet

This T-shaped island to the southeast of Bangkok is well known to students of Thai literature as a setting for the classical epic *Phra Aphaimani* by Sunthon Phu. In Thailand's 1980s economic boom, the 13-sq km (5-sq mile) island began receiving its first visitors, who were more interested in sand and sea than in literature, as young Bangkokians made it a popular weekend retreat. Although the northeastern coast is now crowded with inexpensive resorts, the central and southern shores offer a series of clean, uncrowded white beaches.

Candlelight Beach on Ko Samet

To get to Ko Samet, take the public bus from Ekamai Bus Station in Bangkok to Ban Phe pier. The boat journey from Ban Phe to Ko Samet takes about 45 minutes. Parts of the island come under the jurisdiction of Laem Ya–Ko Samet National Marine Park, and all visitors must pay a fee on arrival. The park's main office is near Hat Sai Kaew, a smaller one is at Ao Wong Deuan. During Thailand's annual southwest monsoon (June–Nov), Ko Samet's east coast is shielded from the heavier rains, so it is popular all year round. Ko Samet can be especially busy during Thai public holidays (see page 117).

Boat tours around Ko Samet and neighbouring islands, including to the Turtle Conservation Centre on Ko Man Nai, are popular. Snorkelling and diving excursions can also be taken.

WHAT TO DO

SHOPPING

In terms of sheer variety and value, Bangkok offers some of Asia's best shopping experiences. From the cramped vendor stalls of local markets to the chic boutiques of Southeast Asia's largest super-mall, you will easily find enough shopping options to keep you busy from dawn to midnight.

Markets

Chatuchak Weekend Market (Sat–Sun 8am–6pm), in the northern part of the city adjacent to Chatuchak Park, is the granddaddy of all Bangkok markets, a conglomeration of over 8,000 stalls purveying practically everything that can be legally sold in Thailand. This market Disneyland is a particularly good hunting ground for second-hand books, design accessories, handicrafts, beads, Thai music CDs, religious amulets, clothing from India and Nepal, military surplus gear and household goods. Bargaining is definitely the order of the day. If hunger strikes, there are plenty of inexpensive but high-quality Thai restaurants. Arrive as early in the morning as possible to avoid the crowds and heat.

Opposite Lumphini Park *(see page 65)*, the **Suan Lum Night Bazaar** (daily 6pm–midnight), in Central Bangkok, has the advantage of being open at night when it is cooler. Hundreds of open-air stalls hawk everything from hill-tribe crafts to gems. Although the market's lease ran out in 2007, it has continued to trade.

Bangkok's infamous backpacker centre, **Khao San Road** *(see page 52)*, has developed a bustling street market dur-

Patpong by night

Thai woodcarver

ing its lengthy reign as Asia's most popular travel stopover. During the day vendors are confined to the pavements on either side of the road, but at night, when Khao San Road is closed to vehicles, they spill into the street, along with *phat thai* (fried rice noodles) carts and VW vans converted into cocktail bars. Dreadlocked merchants specialise in inexpensive beach and travel clothing, luggage and travel accessories, costume jewellery, original-design T-shirts, pirate CDs and DVDs and hair extensions.

A more dense array of market stalls line the two parallel roads of **Patpong** (daily 5pm–midnight, *see page 68*), more famous for its go-go bars, massage parlours and sex shows. Here the selection confines itself to tourist clothing, fake designer watches and handbags, pirate CDs and DVDs (both porn and non-porn) and mainstream Thai souvenirs. Not far away, **Soi Lalai Sap**, the 'money-melting soi' at Soi 5, Silom Road, is a favourite after-lunch stop for local office workers shopping for inexpensive clothing, watches, electronics and housewares.

The **Phahurat** *(see page 37)* and **Chinatown** *(see page 35)* districts have interconnected lanes lined with hundreds of vendors selling well-priced Thai, Indian and Chinese fabrics, along with clothes and accessories, gems and jewellery. The

Wong Wian Yai Market in Thonburi, next to the large roundabout directly southwest of Memorial Bridge, is another all-purpose market, and one that rarely sees tourists.

Spreading over several blocks along Chakraphong, Phra Sumen, Tanao and Rambutri roads, not far from Khao San Road, **Banglamphu Market** is one of the city's most comprehensive shopping districts, as it encompasses everything from street vendors to budget department stores. The area offers better-than-average value on clothing, foodstuffs (including packaged Thai curry pastes) and household items, but there is not much to be found in the way of souvenirs and handicrafts.

The **Maharat Amulet Market** (daily 8am–6pm), occupying several narrow lanes off Maharat Road, opposite Wat Mahathat, offers row upon row of large glass cases filled with sacred amulets (*phra khreuang* in Thai). Each flat piece – usually triangle-shaped – is imprinted with an image of the Buddha, Ganesha, a highly venerated Buddhist monk, or other holy entity. Depending on the amulet and its provenance, the images are said to offer protection against accident and injury, or to further one's career or personal charisma. Prices range from as little as 50 baht for ordinary amulets to tens of thousands of baht for those that are thought to have strong magical powers. Full-size standing and seated Buddha images are also for sale here. Another amulet market can be found at **Wat Ratchanatda**, which is near Mahakan Fort *(see page 50)*.

Traditional cures

Elsewhere along Maharat Road near Wat Mahathat are several traditional Thai medicine shops. The proprietors offer both commercially prepared and custom-blended medicines, most made from natural herbs and plants following age-old Thai and Chinese recipes. Aromatic massage oils are also available, and a few of the shops offer traditional Thai massage.

Shopping Centres and Department Stores

In Bangkok you can barely travel more than half a kilometre without passing a shopping centre or department store. Many are concentrated in the area around Siam Square, a favourite shopping district for Bangkokians, and along nearby Ploenchit and Sukhumvit roads.

Siam Paragon (www.siamparagon.co.th), Southeast Asia's largest mall, corrals half a million square metres of potential purchases. State-of-the-art boutiques stock the latest designer fashions, home furnishings and consumer electronics, while the mall's own **Paragon Department Store** occupies parts of several floors. Gourmet food centres abound, and entertainment options include the Siam Paragon IMAX and Cineplex, Siam World Aquarium and the Siam Opera Theatre.

Emporium Shopping Centre, on Sukhumvit Road and Soi 24, was Bangkok's crown jewel of shopping before Siam

The hustle and bustle of the Mahboonkrong Centre

Paragon came along. It's still a noteworthy stopover for its many European and Thai designer clothing boutiques, interior design shops, upmarket food centre, Kinokuniya bookshop and a cineplex.

Gaysorn Plaza is the place to go for Thai modern design culture. Particularly noteworthy is Fashion Society, which carries a collection of local couture, and single-designer shops Issue, Good Mixer and Sarit. Original furniture and home accessories inspired by traditional Thai design can be found at Ayodhya, Triphum and Maya Ethnic Craft. Meanwhile, Harnn and Thann sells lotions, creams and other personal care products made with local herbs and spices.

H1, a smaller affair on trendy Soi Thong Lor (Soi 55), Sukhumvit Road, is a high-concept shopping centre featuring interconnected glass-and-steel modules, where you can buy retro-modern furniture, design accessories and coffee-table books on art and design, along with a couple of chic restaurants.

Siam Centre was built on crown property in 1976 as Thailand's first shopping mall. It features designer and brand-label clothing shops, as well as boutique opticians, coffee shops and restaurants. Frequent refurbishing has helped Siam Centre maintain its *au courant* image. Connected by an enclosed pedestrian bridge, **Siam Discovery Centre** contains yet more designer stores, supplemented with a half-dozen home interior shops on the fourth floor, including Habitat and Panta, and ground-floor coffee shops.

MBK (Mahboonkrong) Centre, across from Siam Discovery Centre, is one of the capital's most varied and affordable shopping venues. Anchored by the middle-class **Tokyu** department store, MBK packs in hundreds of small shops and hallway vendor stalls selling bargain-priced clothing, photographic equipment and consumer electronics, along with perhaps the largest selection of mobile (cell) phones in Bangkok.

Siam Square, opposite Siam Centre, is made up of 12 *soi* (lanes) that are lined with large and small shops offering books, sporting goods, casual clothing and antiques, along with a branch of Bangkok Bank, several money-exchange booths, travel agencies, cinemas and restaurants. Tucked away in smaller, pedestrian-only *soi* are small shops owned and operated by up-and-coming local designers. Their ready-to-wear clothes often reflect the latest world fashion trends, but tagged with bargain-basement prices.

Central Department Store, Thailand's largest and best department store chain, has 12 branches in Bangkok. The flagship store on Ploenchit Road, near the Chid Lom BTS station, is the largest and most upmarket. In addition to designer clothing, Western cosmetics, fabrics, furniture, hand-

Thai Tailors

Bangkok's many tailor shops can design, cut and sew shirts, dresses, trousers, suits and just about any other article of clothing. Workmanship ranges from shoddy to excellent, so shop around. Most single-piece items, such as a jacket, simple dress, shirt or trousers, can be finished in 48 hours or less with only one fitting. For something more complicated like a suit, the more reputable tailors will ask for two to five sittings.

Bangkok tailors are also adept at copying examples provided by their customers, whether from the original item or a photo. Custom-made shirts or dresses can be knocked off for not much more than a tenth of the designer price.

Thai and Chinese silks are a popular and reasonably priced choice of fabric. Most of the 'cotton' offered by Bangkok tailors is actually a blend of cotton and a synthetic, so bring your own if you want to be assured of 100 percent cotton. 'Special deals' advertising four shirts, two suits, a kimono and a safari suit all in one package almost always turn out to be of inferior materials and workmanship.

Thai silk is available in many beautiful colours

icrafts and attached supermarket, the store offers free alteration on all clothing purchases and free delivery to Bangkok hotels. There's also a fix-it area for watch, shoe and clothing repair. Central's lower-priced subsidiary, **Robinsons**, also has branches throughout the city.

River City Complex, a four-storey shopping centre on the Chao Phraya River next to the Royal Orchid Sheraton, has quality art and antique shops on the third and fourth floors.

Silom Village Trade Centre, on Silom Road, contains less expensive shops selling art, antiques and handicrafts. Here Artisan's specialises in reproduction antique Thai furniture made from recycled teak.

Books

Bangkok offers the best selection of English-language books and bookshops in Southeast Asia. **Asia Books** (Central World Plaza; Emporium; Peninsula Plaza; Siam Discovery Centre;

Sukhumvit Road near Soi 15), **Bookazine** (Siam Square; Silom Complex; Sukhumvit Road between Soi 3 and Soi 5) and **Kinokuniya** (Siam Paragon; Emporium) are the largest chains, with branches sprinkled around Central Bangkok. The independent **Teck Heng Bookstore** (1326 Charoen Krung Road), between the Shangri-La and Oriental hotels, carries an excellent variety of new books on Southeast Asia.

Elite Used Books (593/5 Sukhumvit Road near Soi 33/1) carries a good selection of second-hand titles. Several smaller shops and street vendors along Khao San Road sell second-hand paperback novels and guidebooks.

Antiques

Genuine Thai antiques are rare and costly, and most Bangkok antique shops nowadays supplement their collection of coveted Thai pieces with antiques from neighbouring Myanmar, Laos and China, along with traditionally crafted items made to resemble antiques. The majority of shop operators are candid about what's truly old and what isn't. Good buys include Thai-style furniture made with old teak salvaged from abandoned homes and rice barns. Note that antique Buddha images may not be taken out of the country, and even new images (other than amulets) require a permit from the Department of Fine Arts (tel: 0 2226 1661).

ENTERTAINMENT

In their round-the-clock search for *sanuk* (fun), Bangkokians have made their metropolis one that virtually never sleeps. For an idea of what's on, check the daily entertainment listings in the *Bangkok Post* and *The Nation*. For dance club information log on to Bangkok Spin (www.bangkokspin.com), and for live music happenings, check the Bangkok Gig Guide (www.bangkokgigguide.com).

Theatre

Known in Thai as Sala Chalerm Krung, the **Chalermkrung Royal Theatre** (Old Siam Plaza, corner of Charoen Krung and Triphet roads; tel: 0 2222 0434) is one of Bangkok's top venues for *khon* (classical masked dance-drama). The 1933 Thai Deco cinema was renovated in the 1990s and now has an 80,000-watt audio system. This, combined with superb costuming, set design, dancing and music, enables the 170-member dance troupe to present an authentic yet technologically up-to-date show. Performances last two hours with an interval.

Bamboo dance demonstration

The newer **Siam Niramit Theatre** (Tiam Ruammit Road, opposite the Thailand Cultural Centre; tel: 0 2649 9222; www.siamniramit.com) presents a more technologically enhanced version of *khon* on a huge stage, using laser-based special effects; more than 150 performers run through up to 500 costumes in a performance.

Bars

Of the many international hotel bars, the Conrad Bangkok's **Diplomat Bar** stands out with convenient lobby access, sepia lighting and a relaxed yet sophisticated atmosphere. For an unparalleled nightscape view, sidle up to the curved **Sky Bar,** perched high above the city in the outdoor Sirocco restaurant,

Patpong's finest

on the 63rd floor of the State Tower on Silom Road.

One of the city's most fabulous and longest running watering holes, **Wong's Place** (27/3 Soi Si Bamphen, Rama I Road), caters to both expats and local Thais. Not that far away is the slick and contemporary **Moon Bar** at Vertigo (Banyan Tree, 21/100 Sathon Thai Street, Silom), an open-air bar on the top of a skyscraper.

Newly arrived backpackers sip draught beer and shoot pool at the Khao San Road's popular **Gulliver's Traveller's Tavern**. A second branch can be found in Soi 11, Sukhumvit Road. British-style taverns serving draught beer and pub grub include **Jool's** (Soi 4), **Ship Inn** (Soi 23) and **Bull's Head** (Soi 33/1), all off Sukhumvit Road. Twentysomething Thais party at **Susie Pub**, in an alley off the north side of Khao San, and its sister **Austin Pub** down another alley off the south side. **Taksura** (156/1 Tanao Street) in an old mansion nearby attracts a young arty crowd.

Dance Clubs/DJ Scene

Transplanted from Ho Chi Minh City in 1999, **Q Bar** (www.qbarbangkok.com) is tucked away in a curved-front building towards the back of Soi 11, Sukhumvit Road. The three Ms – models, media and moghuls – are to be seen here, while rotating international DJs spin everything from house to hip-hop.

Also on Soi 11, **Bed Supperclub** (www.bedsupperclub.com) resembles a futuristic spaceship standing on spindly legs. Inside, one half of the building is decorated entirely in white, with wide banks of bed-like sofas on two levels reserved for dinner (the food is outstanding). Meanwhile the back half, plunged into near-darkness, is dedicated to a huge dance floor and DJ booths. Wednesday is Models Night, when the professionally beautiful drink for free while the rest of Bangkok enjoys the view.

The most happening club, and the best sound system in town is at **Club Culture** (www.club-culture-bkk.com; Sri Ayuthaya Road). Right at the centre of Patpong is **Lucifer** (www.luciferdisko.com) which heats up after 11pm. **Café Democ**, off Ratchadamnoen Road near the Democracy Monument, remains one of the city's more casually deco-

Go-Go Bars

Bangkok's world-famous red-light scene is legally restricted to four main areas of the city. The oldest and most well-known district, Patpong (named after its billionaire Thai-Chinese owner), consists of two adjacent pedestrian-only lanes extending between Silom and Surawong roads and lined with bright neon signs advertising go-go bars and 'live shows'. Stalls selling cheap souvenirs and fake designer goods fill the centre of Patpong 2 at night. Nearby Soi Pratuchai and Soi Anuman Ratchathon feature similarly themed bars directed towards gay males.

Soi Cowboy, stretching between Soi 21 and Soi 23, Sukhumvit Road, offers a strip of around 30 hostess and go-go bars. Not far away on Soi 4, Sukhumvit Road, Nana Entertainment Plaza crams around 45 go-go bars into a U-shaped, three-storey complex.

A fourth area, Ratchada, along four-lane Ratchadaphisek Road in the Huay Khwang district in northeast Bangkok, mostly caters to a visiting Japanese and Chinese clientele with mega-large entertainment centres containing massage parlours, hostess bars and karaoke lounges.

rated dance clubs, and an important proving ground for up-and-coming Thai DJs.

Live Music

Bangkok's live music scene ebbs and flows around a number of reliable, long-running venues. **Saxophone Pub** (3/8 Victory Monument, Phayathai Road; www.saxophonepub.com), just off the Victory Monument roundabout, offers a schedule that alternates nightly between blues, jazz and R&B.

In the northern part of the city, **Ruang Pung Art Community** (Sat–Sun 11am–10pm) is a casual open-air affair next to Chatuchak Weekend Market, where the music menu runs from Thai folk-rock to blues.

The city's most famous jazz venue, **Brown Sugar**, is a small but sophisticated bar on Soi Sarasin across from Lumphini Park. The Sunday night jams draw some of the best jazz musicians in Bangkok, including touring jazz pros from abroad.

The city's most elegant jazz club, The Oriental's legendary **Bamboo Bar**, hosts visiting jazz singers fronting the house jazz band. The Sheraton Grand's **Living Room** is another hotel lounge hosting world-class jazz musicians.

In northern Banglamphu, the cryptically named **Ad Here the 13th** (13 Samsen Road, near Soi 1) features some of the capital's most authentic blues playing in a long, narrow bar with a

Late-night venues

Although in the early 2000s the Thaksin administration began enforcing 1am and 2am bar and club closings, places with a restaurant licence are permitted to stay open 24 hours. This means that all-night *khao tom* (rice soup) joints have become very popular, especially along Ratchadaphisek Road in Huay Khwang district. Unlicensed, underground discos, packed from 2am to dawn, change location monthly. Any night-time taxi driver will know the latest hotspots.

Live jazz at the Saxophone Pub

steady Thai and expat following. Another excellent venue for blues is the larger and more modern – but just as soulful – **Tokyo Joe's** (25/9 Soi 26, Sukhumvit Road) near the Emporium Shopping Centre.

The **Brick Bar** in the basement of the Buddy Lodge on Khao San Road has a varied program of live acts attracting a mostly Thai crowd.

Cinema
Multiplex cinemas showing Thai films and the latest blockbusters can be found in nearly every neighbourhood. The highest concentration of cinemas, and those with the best sound systems and most comfortable seating, is in Central Bangkok near Siam Square, in Siam Paragon and the MBK Centre. **EGV**, **Major** and **SF** are the top chains. **House** (UMG Cinema, RCA, Rama IX Road, www.houserama.com) and **Lido Multiplex** (Siam Square) specialise in independent films.

SPORT

Muay Thai

Thailand's national sport, the ancient art of Thai kickboxing *(muay thai)*, is practised at several government-owned stadiums in and around Bangkok. Most centrally located – and the two most foreign visitors frequent – are **Lumphini Boxing Stadium** (Rama IV Road near Withayu Road; www.muaythailumpini.com) and **Ratchadamnoen Boxing Stadium** (Ratchadamnoen Nok Road, next to the TAT information office). The typical fight roster presents eight fights of five rounds each. Admission fees vary according to seating. Ratchadamnoen fights take place on Monday, Wednesday and Thursday from 6.30pm, and on Sunday from 5pm. Lumphini bouts are held Tuesday and Friday from 6.30pm, and on Saturday from 5pm. The best matches are reserved

Thai kickboxing

for Thursday nights at Ratchadamnoen and Tuesday nights at Lumphini. The government has announced that Lumphini Boxing Stadium will eventually be moved to the Suan Phlu district, but so far no date has been announced.

Takraw

In *takraw* several players stand in a circle (the size of the circle depends on the number of players) and try to keep a 12cm (5in) rattan ball aloft by kicking it from one player to another, earning points for style and technique. A more modern variation uses a volleyball court, and is played much like volleyball (with only the feet and head allowed to touch the ball). In yet another variation, players kick the ball into a loosely woven hoop suspended 4.5m (15ft) above the ground. Regular matches are held at the **National Stadium** (Rama I Road), in **Lumphini Park** *(see page 65)* and on school grounds and university campuses throughout the city.

Other Sports

In Thailand **golf** is a sport for the wealthy, and with so much wealth concentrated in Bangkok, there are plenty of well-groomed 18-hole golf courses around the city in adjacent provinces such as Pathum Thani and Chonburi. Most provide transport (at additional cost) from Bangkok with a reserved tee-off. Among the best are Windsor Park Golf Course (42 Mu 8, Suwintawong Road, Kokfat, Nong Chok, tel: 0 2989 4200, www.windsorgolf.co.th), Bangkok Golf Spa Resort (99 Tiwanon Road, Pathum Thani, tel: 0 2501 2828, www.golf.th.com), President Country Club (42 Mu 8, Suwinthawong Road, Nong Chok, tel: 0 2988 7555, www.president.co.th) and Subhapruek Golf Club (Km 26, Bang Na-Trat Highway, tel: 0 2317 0801). The members-only Royal Bangkok Sports Club (Henri Dunant Road) has an 18-hole course right in the city centre – convenient if you are invited by a member.

Tennis courts open to the public include Central Sports Club Tennis Court (13 Soi 1, Sathon Tai Road; tel: 0 2213 1909) and Santisuk Tennis Courts (Sukhumvit Road between Soi 36 and Soi 38).

Horse racing takes place at Royal Turf Club of Thailand (Phitsanulok Road; tel: 0 2280 0020) and Royal Bangkok Sports Club (Henri Dunant Road; tel: 0 2251 0181) on alternate Sundays, 12.30am–6pm.

CHILDREN'S BANGKOK

Bangkok has plenty of activities for children. For a start there is the Dusit Zoo *(see page 59)*, Snake Farm *(see page 64)*, Lumphini Park *(see page 65)* and Samut Prakan Crocodile Farm and Zoo *(see page 71)*. The Children's Discovery Museum (Queen Sirikit Park; Tue–Fri 9am–5pm, Sat–Sun 10am–6pm; tel: 0 2615 6509), adjacent to Chatuchak Weekend Market, offers hands-on exhibits on nature, the environment and science, plus a playground around the back.

Siam Ocean World (www.siamoceanworld.com; Siam Paragon, Rama I Road; daily 9am–10pm) is South East Asia's largest oceanarium with huge numbers of ocean dwelling species including sharks and penguins.

At the Snake Farm

Outside Bangkok **Siam Park** (99 Seri Thai Road, Kanna Yao; daily 10am–6pm; tel: 0 2919 7200; www.siam parkcity.com) has a water park with wave pools, a bird park with aviaries, plus a children's playground, as well as botanical gardens.

Calendar of Events

Dates for Buddhist festivals vary from year to year in accordance with Thailand's traditional lunar calendar.

January–February *River of Kings:* 12 days of impressive sound-and-light shows, along with Thai dance and music, at Ratchaworadit Pier on the Chao Phraya River.

Chinese New Year (date varies from year to year): Chinatown brings in the new year with lion dances and fireworks.

February–March *Magha Puja* (full moon of the third lunar month): commemoration of an apocryphal tale in 1250 when monks turned up to hear the Buddha preach without a prior announcement. A candlelit walk to the summit of the Golden Mount is a highlight.

13–15 April *Songkhran Festival:* Thailand's traditional new year celebration involves pouring water over an image of the Buddha and over monks and community elders. In the streets, Thais throw water from bowls or buckets onto passers-by during the daytime; once night falls, everything returns to normal.

May *Visakha Puja* (15th day of the waxing moon in the sixth lunar month): this important day celebrates the Buddha's birth, enlightenment and *parinibbana*; candlelit processions and chanting in Buddhist monasteries.

Royal Ploughing Ceremony: an ancient Brahmanic ritual, in which rice seed is ceremonially sowed at Sanam Luang just before the rainy season to bring good rains to farmers; the king presides over the ceremony, which attracts thousands of Thais.

July *Asalha Puja:* a day honouring the Buddha's first sermon; Theravada Buddhist temples in the capital host hold candlelit processions.

September–October *Vegetarian Festival* (first nine days of ninth lunar month): an orgy of vegetarian food in Chinatown for nine days.

November *Loi Krathong* (full moon of the 12th lunar month): small lotus-shaped floats are loaded with flowers, incense, candles and a coin, and then launched on Bangkok's rivers and canals.

5 December *King's Birthday:* celebrations include an elaborate parade on Ratchadamnoen Klang Avenue.

EATING OUT

Bangkok lures more visitors than any other capital in Southeast Asia not only because of its spectacular temples and renowned nightlife but also because it has one of the most robust and varied cuisines in the region. Whether following carefully preserved royal Thai recipes or inspired by the latest Mediterranean fusion cooking techniques, Bangkok's cooks can collectively boast a vast arsenal of tongue-tempting delights.

WHERE TO EAT

You can't walk more than a few metres in the capital without coming across a street stall, a cluster of tables on the pavement, or a restaurant. Most dining venues in Bangkok's tourist districts offer menus in English, but in places where there are no English menus there's usually someone who can help you order. Many restaurants have their own house specialities in addition to what's listed on the menu, so it's worth asking the waiter for recommendations.

Economical places to eat include noodle shops *(raan kuaytiaw)*, curry-rice shops *(raan khao kaeng)*, food centres *(suun aahaan)* and night markets *(ta-laat toh rung)*. In addition to being inexpensive, the dishes served at such places are invariably delicious and very authentic. Some of

Budget grub

Backpackers can find plenty to please both the palate and the pocket on and around Khao San Road in Banglamphu. Night markets such as the Soi 38 Night Market (Soi 38, Sukhumvit Road) and Suan Luang Night Market (Soi 5, Ban That Thong, near Chulalongkorn University) feature cheap yet marvellously authentic Thai dishes.

the best and cheapest food can be found at food stalls lining the streets. Vendors buy their ingredients fresh from the market in the early morning and prepare their dishes before your very eyes.

At a curry-rice shop *(raan khao kaeng)*, pots of curry will be placed on a table towards the front of the shop, along with a large rice cooker. Typically the pots will not be sitting on a stove or heating element of any kind. The curries are cooked early in the morning till piping hot, and once lidded they will stay warm for a few hours. Curry-rice shops open early in the morning and usually close by 2pm.

Rooftop dining at the Sirocco restaurant, State Tower building

At the other end of the scale, luxury hotel restaurants offer some of the city's best haute cuisine, whether Thai or international. Among the best of the five-star hotel dining venues are those found at The Oriental, Four Seasons, The Metropolitan and The Conrad Bangkok.

International dining options in Bangkok are rich and varied, with every major Asian and Western cuisine well covered. Chinese food is naturally best in Bangkok's **Chinatown**, Indian food in the Indian-dominated neighbourhoods of **Phahurat** and **Bangrak**, and Middle Eastern in the **Nana** neighbourhood off Sukhumvit Road. Sukhumvit is also your best bet for Italian and French cuisines.

Traditional sauces accompany many dishes

WHAT TO EAT

Thai Cooking

Bangkok cuisine relies heavily on fresh ingredients. Fresh vegetables, poultry, pork and beef are the main ingredients, usually cooked quickly by stir-frying, steaming or par-boiling. Fresh lime juice, kaffir lime leaves, lemongrass and coriander leaf are added to give the food its characteristic tang, while fish sauce *(naam plaa)* or shrimp paste *(ka-pi)* contribute salty tones.

Three members of the ginger family – galangal *(khaa)*, ginger *(khing)* and turmeric *(kha-min)* – also find their way into many dishes. In addition, cooks season the food with black pepper, three kinds of basil, ground peanuts (more often a condiment), tamarind juice and coconut milk.

Some Thai dishes can be very spicy, particularly those containing fresh *phrik khee nuu*, small torpedo-shaped bird chillies which timid eaters may want to push aside. Less spicy dishes use dried chilli flakes and a few contain no chillies at all.

Rice *(khao)* is eaten with most meals, and in fact the Thai phrase 'to eat' is *kin khao*, literally 'eat rice'. There are many varieties and grades of rice, with the finest known as *khao hawm mali* or 'jasmine-scented rice' for its sweet, inviting smell when cooked.

Combining coconut cream, fresh-pounded chillies, ginger, garlic and onions, Thai curries *(kaeng)* are among the hottest in the world. They come in several varieties, including red curry *(kaeng phet)*, green curry *(kaeng khiaw-waan)* and mild peanut-based curry *(kaeng phanaeng)*. Most fiery of all is the 'jungle curry' *(kaeng paa)*, which dispenses with the coconut cream for a pure chilli base.

Stir-fried dishes are the most popular choice among Bangkokians. Favourites include *phat bai ka-phrao* (chicken or pork stir-fried with basil, garlic, fresh chilli and soy sauce), *kai phat phrik khing* (chicken stir-fried with ginger and dried red chilli) and *kai phat met ma-muang himaphaan* (sliced chicken stir-fried with cashews and dried chilli).

Another Thai staple is *yam*, a hot, tangy salad made with a mixture of fresh and cooked ingredients. One of the most common is *yam plaa duk fuu*, which tosses together fried grated catfish, fresh chopped chilli and peanuts, served with a spicy/salty/sour green mango dressing on the side.

Two of the most common Thai soups are fiery *tom yam* (spicy lemongrass soup, usually made with seafood) and less spicy *tom kha* (spicy coconut cream and galangal soup, usu-

Eating Thai-Style

Most Thai dishes are eaten with a fork *(sawm)* and tablespoon *(chawn)*. Proper etiquette dictates that you eat with the spoon, the fork being used only to prod the food onto the spoon. Chopsticks *(ta-kiap)* are used only when eating in Chinese restaurants or for eating noodle dishes.

Thai meals are shared among the diners and served from common serving platters in the centre of the table. When taking food from a common platter, you place only one spoonful at a time onto your plate.

Typically the table orders one of each kind of dish, for example, one spicy dish, one mild dish, one fish dish, one soup and so on. One or two extra dishes will be ordered when there are four or more diners.

Many restaurants will have a separate *jaan diaw* (one-plate dish) section on the menu listing rice and noodle dishes. Solo diners can also order dishes over rice *(raat khao)*.

ally served with filleted chicken). They are served with steamed rice to soak up the excess chilli heat.

Smaller dishes meant to be eaten while drinking alcoholic beverages are called *kap klaem*. Some Thai menus translate these as 'snacks' or 'appetisers'. Typical *kap klaem* include fried peanuts *(thua thawt)* and spicy cashew salad *(yam met ma-muang himaphaan)*.

Noodles come in two basic varieties, white rice noodles *(kuaytiaw)* and yellow wheat noodles *(ba-mee)*. Either can be ordered in a soup *(naam)*, or as steamed noodles without broth *(haeng)* or stir-fried *(phat)* with other ingredients. One can choose between several meats, most commonly chicken, pork and beef, with seafood an occasional option.

Thais rarely order desserts or pastries at the end of a meal, but rather freshly sliced fruit. Pineapple, papaya, watermelon, mandarin orange, guava, mango and banana are the most commonly served fruits, but diners may also come across star-fruit and pomelo. The infamous durian – known as the 'king

The Bomb

Dubbed the king of fruits by the Thais, yet despised by many foreigners, the durian *(thurian* in Thai) belongs to the *Bombacaceae* family and is native only to Southeast Asia. The heavy, spiked shell holds five sections of kidney-shaped, yellow-coloured flesh. One of the most well-known descriptions of the fruit is by 19th-century British scientist Alfred Russell Wallace:

'Custard flavoured with almonds, intermingled with wafts of flavour that call to mind cream cheese, onion sauce, brown sherry and other incongruities… neither acid, nor sweet, nor juicy, yet one feels the want of none of these qualities for it is perfect as it is.'

Due to its strong odour, most Bangkok hotels, as well as all domestic and international airlines, prohibit the fruit from their premises.

of fruits' for its rich and creamy texture – has such a strong smell that it is very rarely served in restaurants. Instead durians are bought from street vendors or in fresh markets, then eaten outdoors or at home.

International Cuisines

Almost any world cuisine you can name can be found somewhere in Bangkok, including Chinese, Mexican, British, Cajun-Creole, Japanese, Korean, French, Italian, Indian, Spanish, German, Arabic and Swedish. Italian cooking is particularly well represented, with some rest-aurants even specialising in

Seafood dish

Tuscan, Sardinian and other regional styles. The city has some stellar Indian restaurants as well.

Although it originally hails from Japan, *sukiyaki* has taken on many Thai characteristics in Bangkok, where it's extremely popular. *Sukee* (as it's called in Thai) is found in restaurants where booths or round tables are centred around a large pot sitting on a gas burner. The pot is filled with a broth at the beginning of the meal and, once it's boiling, diners sitting around the pot begin adding raw ingredients – *wun sen* (cellophane noodles), egg, water spinach, cabbage, thinly sliced beef and seafood – to the hot broth using chopsticks. When cooked, the diners then dip them into a Japanese-influenced sesame-chilli-garlic sauce.

Locals dining out

WHAT TO DRINK

Non-Alcoholic Beverages

All restaurants serve purified water, whether by the glass or by the bottle. Thai restaurants also offer a variety of juices and fruit shakes made from Thailand's abundant fresh fruits, including most commonly mandarin orange, watermelon, pineapple, guava, papaya, mango, sugar cane and, best of all, fresh coconut water served straight from the coconut.

Alcoholic Drinks

Thai-owned breweries produce a number of locally sold beers, including both domestic brands and licensed international brands. Singha, the country's oldest and most well-known label, packs a punch at 6 percent alcohol, outdone only by less expensive Chang (7 percent). Dutch giant Heineken, which co-operates a brewery just outside Bangkok, ranks third in sales after Singha and Chang. Various imported beers – everything from Mexico's Corona to Ireland's Guinness – can be found in the city's more upmarket bars and restaurants. Draught beer (*bia sot*, literally 'fresh beer') is available in many Bangkok pubs and restaurants.

Sangsom, a popular and inexpensive 'whisky' (actually made with sugar cane, so technically a rum) made in Thailand, has an alcoholic content of 35 percent and is popular with working-class Thais and university students. Spey Royal and 100 Pipers cost a bit more and are distilled to resemble the taste of malt whisky. Thai whiskies are almost always ordered by the bottle. Some restaurants offer a special price for ordering a set that includes a bottle of whisky, ice and mixers.

Wine has become very popular in Bangkok over the last decade or so, and imported wines from France, Italy, the US, Australia and Chile are commonly available in wine shops and many restaurants. Thailand also produces its own wine, of which the Monsoon Valley and GranMonte labels are well worth trying.

To Help You Order…

Do you have …?	**Mee … mai?**
I eat only vegetarian food.	**Chan kin jeh.**
Not spicy.	**Mai phet.**
The bill, please.	**Kep taang duay.**
I'd like a/an/some …	**Khaw …**

beer	**bia**	iced coffee	**kaa-fae yen**
cup	**thuay**	iced tea	**chaa yen**
fork	**sawm**	fruit	**phon-la-mai**
glass	**kaew**	menu	**meh-noo**
hot coffee	**kaa-fae rawn**	spoon	**chawn**
hot tea	**chaa rawn**	steamed rice	**khao suay**
ice	**naam khaen**	water	**naam**

...and Read the Menu

kaeng khiaw-waan kai	green curry with chicken
kaeng phet kai/neua	red curry with chicken/beef
kai phat bai ka-phrao	chicken stir-fried with hot chillies
kai phat khing	chicken stir-fried with ginger and mild chillies
kai phat met ma-muang himaphaan	chicken stir-fried with dried chillies and cashews
kai thawt	fried chicken
kai yaang	grilled chicken
khai dao	fried egg
khai jiaw	Thai-style omelette
khao phat kai/moo	fried rice with chicken/pork
khao tom moo/kung	rice soup with pork/prawns
kluay thawt	batter-fried bananas
kuaytiaw phat see-yu	stir-fried rice noodles
kung phao	grilled prawns
moo krawp	crisp-fried pork
moo yang	grilled pork
naam kluay pan	banana shake
naam taeng-moh pan	watermelon shake
phat phak	stir-fried vegetables
phat phak buay leng	stir-fried Chinese spinach
phat phak bung fai daeng	water spinach stir-fried with chillies, garlic and soy sauce
phat thai	rice noodles stir-fried with tofu, bean sprouts, egg, dried shrimp
phrik naam plaa	chillies in fish sauce
som-tam	spicy green papaya salad
tom kha kai	galangal and coconut soup with chicken
tom yam khung	spicy lemongrass soup with prawns
yam plaa duk foo	spicy catfish salad
yam plaa meuk	spicy squid salad

HANDY TRAVEL TIPS

An A–Z Summary of Practical Information

A

ACCOMMODATION

(See also RECOMMENDED HOTELS on page 128)

Bangkok accommodation runs the gamut from backpacker guest-houses to world-class luxury hotels. At all price ranges, the city typically offers some of the best value anywhere in Asia. Rates and occupancies run highest during the November–February peak season, and lowest in May, June and September.

Major hotels are predominantly found in several areas of the city. Four- and five-star business hotels are commonly located in the Silom Road financial district, while the higher-end tourist hotels line the Chao Phraya River. Sukhumvit Road in the eastern part of the capital is lined with both middle- and high-end international chain hotels, and is convenient for BTS Skytrain passengers.

Less expensive accommodation tends to be concentrated in Banglamphu close to Khao San Road, but there are also a few up-and-coming boutique hotels in this area. Close to Siam Square are a number of budget and mid-range hotels and guesthouses. The Siam Square area is also easily accessible by BTS.

In northern Bangkok, the Ratchadaphisek neighbourhood is known for larger tourist-class hotels catering primarily to East Asian tourists, and is conveniently reached via the Metro subway.

Web-based booking services often offer special internet rates for Bangkok hotels. Two reliable booking sites with Bangkok listings are www.asiatravel.com and www.res24.com.

single room	**hawng diaw**
double room	**hawng khoo**
I'd like a single/double room with bathroom.	**Tawng-kaan hawng diaw/khoo hawng naam nai tua.**
What's the rate per night?	**Khaa hawng thao rai?**

AIRPORTS

Bangkok has two airports. Approximately 30km (19 miles) east of the city, **Suvarnabhumi Airport** (call centre tel: 0 2132 1888, departures tel: 0 2132 9324, arrivals tel: 0 2132 9328, help desk tel: 0 2132 3888; www.suvarnabhumiairport.com), also known as New Bangkok International Airport (NBIA), replaced Don Muang Airport for all international flights in September 2006. Despite the spelling, the name is pronounced Suwannapoom. When it opened, the new airport boasted the largest terminal and tallest control tower in the world. Several airlines fly direct from Australasia, Europe and the US. An international air departure tax of THB700 per passenger is included in most ticket purchases but is occasionally collected by the carrier at airport check-in.

Suvarnabhumi is linked to the city by a convenient system of elevated highways. Road travel from the airport to most parts of Bangkok averages 30–45 minutes: there are taxis (THB250–350 to most parts of the city) and airport buses (four lines to most parts of the city; 5am–midnight; THB150). A 28km (17-mile) SRT rail link is under construction and expected to open during 2009.

The older **Don Muang Airport** (tel: 0 2535 1192; www2.airport thai.co.th) was originally closed when Suvarnabhumi opened in September 2006, but in March 2007, three Thailand-based airlines shifted domestic services back to Don Muang. Thai Airways International (THAI) operates some domestic flights from Don Muang (but all international flights from Suvarnabhumi). THAI routes which use Don Muang include Phitsanulok, Udon Thani, Ubon Ratchathani and Surat Thani; THAI flights to Chiang Mai, Chiang Rai, Phuket, Hat Yai and Krabi operate via both Don Muang (for non-connecting flights) and Suvarnabhumi (for connecting flights). Two other domestic airlines using Don Muang exclusively are Nok Air and Orient Thai.

For transport into the city (23km/14 miles) from Don Muang, passengers can choose to go by taxi (THB200–350), railway (schedule varies; THB12–39) or public bus (5am–11pm; THB12).

Road transport between the two airports takes a minimum of 30 minutes or, during rush hour traffic, up to an hour. Taxi fare runs around THB380, bus fare THB35.

The government may move all flights back to Suvarnabhumi Airport in the near future, so be sure to confirm airport information with your carrier before flying domestically.

I need a taxi.	**Tawng-kaan rot taek-see.**
How much is it to… ?	**Pai… thao rai?**
Does this bus go to…?	**Rot meh nee pai… mai?**

B

BARGAINING

Prices for goods for sale at markets and street stalls are usually negotiable and bargaining is expected. A genuine smile will go a long way towards obtaining a good price.

I want this one.	**Khaw an-nee.**
Can I look at that one?	**Khaw doo an-nan?**
small/too small	**lek/lek pai**
large/too large	**yai/yai pai**
Let me see another colour please.	**Khaw doo see eun?**
Can you lower the price?	**Lot raakhaa dai mai?**
expensive/too expensive	**phaeng/phaeng pai**
cheap	**thook**

BUDGETING FOR YOUR TRIP

Bangkok is one of Asia's least expensive capitals. The following is meant only as a rough guide. There are approximately THB55 to £1 sterling and THB35 to the US dollar.

Accommodation. Room rates at the average mid-range hotel in popular areas run to approximately THB2,000–3,000 a night. Some hotels add a 10 percent service charge and 7 percent hotel tax (one of the lowest in the region).

Meals and drinks. Breakfast or lunch in a local Thai restaurant runs to no more than THB100 per person, dinner about THB200. A multi-course meal in a mid-range restaurant for tourists costs around THB400 per person, not including alcoholic beverages. Compared to food, alcoholic drinks are pricey in Bangkok: THB60–120 for a 750ml bottle of beer. Owing to the fact that they are heavily taxed, imported liquors and wine are likely to cost much more in Bangkok than in your home country.

Entertainment. Typical museum entry fees are THB40–100. Entry to most Buddhist temples is free, with Wat Pho (THB50), Wat Arun (THB20) and Wat Phra Kaew (THB250) the most notable exceptions. Cinema tickets cost around THB150, and the few dance clubs with cover charges cost around THB300 (including one or two drinks).

Transport. Most metered taxi rides around the city cost under THB150, or to one of the airports THB200–300. Three-wheeled motorcycle taxis called *tuk-tuks* charge about the same as metered taxis, but you must bargain the fare first. Two-wheeled motorcycle taxis in smaller streets charge THB10–20 per ride. City buses charge around THB8–10 for non-air-conditioned routes, otherwise THB10–17. The BTS Skytrain costs THB15–40 depending on distance, while the newer MRTA (Metro) subway is THB16–45.

C

CAR HIRE (RENTAL)

Self-drive car hire isn't recommended in Bangkok's challenging traffic, especially since a car and driver costs about the same as a car alone. Count on THB1,500 per day for a small car and THB2,000–2,500 for something nicer. Most can provide a driver for around THB650–750.

Recommended car-hire companies include:
Avis tel: 0 2255 5300; www.avisthailand.com
Budget tel: 0 2203 9222; www.budget.co.th

I'd like to rent a car tomorrow for one day/week with full insurance.	**Yak ja chao rot yon wan phrung nee neung wan/neung aathit phrawm prakan rot.**

CLIMATE

Bangkok sits on a flat, humid river delta, with tropical temperatures all year round. The southwest monsoon typically sweeps in from the Indian Ocean in May and lasts until mid- to late October. During this season the heaviest rainfall usually occurs during August and September. Beginning in December, rains from a second monsoon from the northeast bypass Bangkok but bring lower relative temperatures until mid-February. With both monsoons gone, much higher relative temperatures follow from March to May before the whole cycle begins again. The following chart shows the average number of rainy days each month:

	J	F	M	A	M	J	J	A	S	O	N	D
Rainy days	2	2	4	5	14	16	19	21	23	17	7	1

CLOTHING

Casual dress is acceptable for almost all occasions in Bangkok. Because of the hot, humid climate, lightweight, breathable fabrics are the most comfortable option. Five-star hotel restaurants frown on shorts or sandals. Shorts (men and women) and plunging necklines are considered culturally unacceptable for Buddhist temple visits. Shoes must be removed before entering Buddhist shrine halls or private homes.

CRIME AND SAFETY (See also EMERGENCIES)

Crime against tourists is relatively rare in Bangkok. None of the city's districts need to be considered 'off limits' for security reasons. Guard your belongings against pickpockets on crowded buses or in markets, and in the Khao San Road area. Avoid any stranger who brings up the topic of gems or tailor shops, as these are virtually always an introduction to a scam.

Call the police!	**Khaw jaeng tam-ruat!**
Help!	**Chuay duay!**
Call a doctor!	**Khaw riak maw!**
Danger!	**Antaraai!**

CUSTOMS AND ENTRY REQUIREMENTS

All foreign visitors to Thailand must carry a passport valid for at least six months after their arrival. Citizens of around 40 countries may visit Thailand for 30 days without any visa (permission to stay is granted on arrival). For visits of more than a month, you should obtain Thailand's 60-day Tourist Visa from a Thai consulate or embassy abroad. For a comprehensive look at visa types visit the Ministry of Foreign Affairs website (www.mfa.go.th).

There are no limitations on the amount of Thai or foreign currency you may bring into the country. The importation of illegal drugs, firearms and pornographic media is forbidden. Visitors may bring one camera, 200 cigarettes and 1 litre of wine or spirits duty-free. Personal stereos, musical instruments and computers are fine as long as you don't carry more than one of each.

Antiques, art and Buddha images acquired in Thailand require an export licence from the Department of Fine Arts (in the National Museum at 4 Na Phra That Road; tel: 0 2226 1661) before they are taken out of the country. Antique Buddha images cannot be taken out at all. The licensing procedure takes three to five days.

E

ELECTRICITY

Thailand's power supply is 220V, 50 cycles. Most wall outlets take dual-pin plugs, both round and flat. Adaptors and voltage converters are available at most hotels or they can be purchased at local shops selling electrical supplies. A majority of hotels have an electrical outlet for shavers; some have 110V sockets, too.

EMBASSIES

Be sure to phone before visiting, as most embassies are open to the public only in the morning or afternoon.

Australia: 37 Sathon Tai Road, tel: 0 2344 6300, www.aust embassy.or.th.

Canada: 15th floor, Abdulrahim Building, 990 Rama IV Road, tel: 0 2636 0540, www.canadainternational.gc.ca/thailand-thailande.

South Africa: 12 A Floor, M-Thai Tower, All Seasons Place, 87 Withayu (Wireless) Road, tel: 0 2659 2900, www.saembbangkok.com.

UK: 14 Withayu (Wireless) Road, tel: 0 2305 8333, www.british embassy.gov.uk/thailand.

US: 120–122 Withayu (Wireless) Road, tel: 0 2205 4000, http:// bangkok.usembassy.gov.

embassy	**sathaan thoot**
passport	**nang seu doen thaang**
visa	**wee-saa**
Where's the British/ American embassy?	**Sathaan thoo angkrit/ amerikaa yoo thee nai?**

EMERGENCIES (See also CRIME AND SAFETY)

Emergency numbers in Bangkok:
Police (and Ambulance) **191**; Tourist Police **1155**; Fire **195**.

G

GAY AND LESBIAN TRAVELLERS

Homosexuality is accepted by most Thais, particularly in Bangkok, and there are no laws forbidding same-sex alliances. The city has the most celebrated gay and lesbian scene in Asia. There are many bars catering for gay men and a smaller number for lesbians. Utopia's website (www.utopia-asia.com) is an excellent source of information for gay and lesbian venues and events in Bangkok.

GETTING THERE (See also AIRPORTS)

Bangkok can only be reached by air or sea.

By air. Suvarnabhumi Airport receives hundreds of international flights daily from cities in Asia, Australia, Europe and the US. The national carrier, Thai Airways International (THAI; tel: 0 2232 8000; www.thaiair.com), has the most extensive route network and flight schedule. Other airlines with frequent direct and non-stop international service to Bangkok include Air Asia, Air Canada, Air France, Air India, Air New Zealand, British Airways, Cathay Pacific, Emirates, Korean Airlines, Japan Airlines, KLM, Lufthansa, Northwest, Qantas, Singapore Airlines and United Airlines.

By sea. There are no regularly scheduled passenger services to Bangkok. Several cruise lines, such as Seabourn (www.seabourn. com), Cunard (www.cunardline.com) and Princess Cruises (www. princess.com), include Bangkok as a port of call.

GUIDES AND TOURS

Day tours. Most hotels and guesthouses can arrange day tours by car or van. Less expensive tours are pre-arranged, while customised tours cost only a little more. The larger hotels have their own tour desks with detailed tour itineraries and staff who can help you select the most appropriate one. Visitors can also contact outside tour operators such as World Travel Service (1053 Charoen Krung Road;

tel: 0 2233 5900; www.wts-thailand.com), which was founded in 1947 and is one of Bangkok's largest agencies.

River and Canal Tours. Boat tours of the Chao Phraya River and the linking canals of Khlong Bangkok Yai, Khlong Bangkok Noi and Khlong Om are a popular way of seeing parts of the city that aren't easily visited by road. Longtail boats moored at Tha Chang, Tha Tien and Tha Banglamphu river piers offer standard and customised river/canal tours for around THB500–800 per hour.

Bicycle Tours. Real Asia (tel: 0 2665 6364; www.realasia.net) offers daily bike trips around Thonburi's canalside districts and gardens.

> We'd like an English-speaking guide/an English interpreter. **Rao yaak dai phoo nam thiaw/laam thee phoot phaasaa thai dai.**

H

HEALTH AND MEDICAL CARE

Thailand requires no vaccinations prior to arrival. Health professionals recommend vaccinations for hepatitis A and B if you plan to stay in Thailand more than a month. Consult the World Health Organisation (www.who.int/en) for any current health warnings for Thailand. Aside from having Thailand's best health-care facilities, Bangkok is a well-known destination for medical tourism.

Hospitals. US-accredited **Bumrungrad International** (33 Soi 3, Sukhumvit Road; tel: 0 2667 1000; www.bumrungrad.com) is the most luxurious hospital complex in the city. Other recommended hospitals include **Mission Hospital** (430 Phitsanulok Road; tel: 0 2282 1100; www.mission-hospital.org), **Samitivej Sukhumvit Hospital** (133 Soi 49, Sukhumvit Road; tel: 0 2711 8000; www.samitivej.co.th) and **Bangkok Hospital** (2 Soi 47, New Phetburi Road; tel: 0 2310 3000; www.bangkokhospital.com). They all offer

24-hour emergency services along with dental and ophthalmological treatment facilities.

Pharmacies. Open 24 hours in hospitals and Foodland Supermarket Pharmacy (1413 Soi 5, Sukhumvit Road; tel: 0 2254 2247).

pharmacy	**raan khaai yaa**
hospital	**rohng phayaabaan**
doctor	**maw**
Where's the nearest pharmacy?	**Raan khaai yaa klai-sut yoo thee nai?**
I need a doctor/dentist.	**Chan tawng-kaan maw/maw fan.**
an ambulance	**rot phayaabaan**
an upset stomach	**thawng sia**
a fever	**pen khai**

HOLIDAYS

Banks and government offices, along with some businesses, are closed on the following public holidays (many are fixed to the lunar calendar so differ each year):

1 January	New Year's Day
January/February	Chinese New Year (first lunar month)
March	Magha Puja (full moon of the third lunar month)
6 April	Chakri Day
May	Vesakha Puja (full moon of the sixth lunar month)
5 May	Coronation Day
July	Asalha Puja (full moon of the eighth lunar month)
	Vassa (day after the full moon)
12 August	Queen's Birthday
23 October	Chulalongkorn Day
5 December	King's Birthday
10 December	Constitution Day

L

LANGUAGE

English is widely used in hotels and shops, but it is always greatly appreciated when visitors try to speak some Thai. Bangkokians speak the Central Thai dialect, one of four major Thai dialects in Thailand. Thai has its own script with 44 consonants and 32 vowels. It's also a tonal language, so the meaning of a word or syllable may be altered by speaking that word with one of five different tones. Thai has five tones: low tone, level or mid tone, falling tone, high tone and rising tone. Depending on the tone, for example, the word *mai* might mean 'new', 'burn', 'wood' or 'not'.

Transliteration of Thai using the Roman alphabet is difficult since there are only a few one-to-one phonological correspondences between Thai and English. The most different include:

k	like the 'k' in 'skin'
kh	like the 'k' in 'kite'
p	like the 'p' in 'stopper' (not the 'p' in 'pat')
ph	like the 'p' in 'pat' (never as the 'ph' in 'phone')
t	like the 't' in 'forty' (not the 't' in 'top')
th	like the 't' in 'top'
ng	like the 'ng' in 'hang', but used as an initial consonant

To be polite, men should end each sentence with the politening syllable *khrap*. Women should end each sentence with *kha*.

MAPS

Free maps are available at hotel reception counters. Detailed city maps may be purchased at bookshops throughout Bangkok. The most useful maps will have entries labelled in both English and Thai.

MEDIA

Newspapers. Two English-language dailies are widely available, *Bangkok Post* and *The Nation*. *The International Herald Tribune* (Singapore edition) can be found in most hotel news-stands.

Listing magazines. Free English-language weekly *BK Magazine* (http://bkmagazine.com) and monthly *Bangkok 101* have good listings and reviews of sights, restaurants and happenings.

MONEY

Currency. The Thai baht (THB) is the national currency. Paper notes are colour-coded and come in denominations of THB20 (green), THB50 (blue), THB100 (red), THB500 (purple) and THB1,000 (brown). 1-, 5- and 10-baht coins are also widely circulated, and the baht is further divided into 100 satang, available as 25-satang and 50-satang coins.

Banks. All Thai banks offer foreign exchange services at branches throughout the city. The most foreigner-friendly are Bank of Ayudhya, Bangkok Bank, KasikornBank and Siam Commercial Bank. Most banks are open Mon–Fri 8.30am–3.30pm, but some branches maintain exchange booths open until 8pm.

Cash dispensers (ATMs). Facilities for using your debit or credit card to withdraw cash automatically function 24 hours a day throughout the city. Most will accept international cards and as such are the most convenient way for foreign visitors to withdraw cash as needed. The exchange rate for cash dispensers is better than the rate at exchange booths, and transaction fees are low.

Credit cards. Visa and MasterCard credit cards are accepted at most hotels and department stores, luxury restaurants and upmarket shops. American Express is less widely accepted. Lost or stolen cards may be reported to:

   American Express: tel: 0 2273 5544.
   MasterCard: tel: 001 800 11 887 0663.
   Visa: tel: 001 800 441 3485.

Currency exchange. Cash dispensers are the most convenient and least costly way to obtain cash in Bangkok, but visitors may also change major foreign currencies (cash or travellers' cheques) at local banks or at bank-owned foreign-exchange booths in Suvarnabhumi Airport and in areas where there are many tourists (such as Sukhumvit, Silom and Khao San roads). Banks and exchange booths charge a commission of up to THB23 for cashing travellers' cheques.

Can I pay with this credit card?	**Jaai pen bat credit yang nee dai mai?**
I want to change some pounds/dollars.	**Yaak ja laek plian pound/dollar.**
Can you cash a travellers' cheque?	**Laek plian chek doen thaang dai mai?**
Where's the nearest bank?	**Thanaakhaan klai-sut yoo thee nai?**
Is there a cash machine near here?	**Mee khreuang atm klai thee nee mai?**
How much is that?	**Nee raakhaa thao rai?**

OPENING HOURS

Banks. Monday–Friday 8.30am–3.30pm. Foreign-exchange booths may stay open until 8pm.

Shops. Most shops are open Monday–Saturday 10am–6pm. Department stores may be open as late as 10pm.

Offices. Government and business offices generally open Monday–Friday 8.30am–4.30pm. Some also open Saturday 8.30am–noon. Most government offices take an unofficial lunch break noon–1pm.

Nightspots. Bars are permitted to stay open until midnight, live music clubs until 1am and discos/dance clubs until 2am.

P

POLICE (See also EMERGENCIES and CRIME AND SAFETY)

The Royal Thai Police wear brown uniforms. They can be reached via a three-digit hotline number, 191. Most members of the police speak very little English.

It is best to report thefts or other criminal complaints to the Tourist Police, a separate, English-speaking force trained to deal with foreigners. The Tourist Police can be reached by dialling 1155 any time of day or night.

police	tam-ruat
Tourist Police	tam-ruat thawng thiaw
Where's the nearest police station?	Sathaanee tam-ruat thee klai-sut yoo thee nai?
I've lost my... wallet/bag/passport.	...haai kra-bao ngoen/ kra-bao/nang seu doen thaang.

POST OFFICES

Bangkok's main post office on Charoen Krung Road is open Monday–Friday 8am–8pm, weekends and holidays 8am–1pm. Branch post offices, open weekdays only, can be found around the city. Almost all the big hotels offer postal services, and newsagents sell stamps.

Thailand's domestic and international postal services are fast, efficient and inexpensive. Most post offices also offer packaging materials and packing services, as well as poste restante mail.

Where's the nearest post office?	Praisanee klai-sut yoo thee nai?
express (special delivery)	ems
registered	long tha-bian

PUBLIC TRANSPORT

Boat. Large longtail boats ply regular routes along a few of Bangkok's canals, much like a water-borne bus service, with fares from THB10–25. The most extensive services are along Khlong Saen Saep, which runs east–west across much of the city from Banglamphu to Bang Kapi, more or less parallel to Sukhumvit Road.

Along the Chao Phraya River, larger cruisers operated by Chao Phraya Express Boat (tel: 2623 6001; fares THB20–35) run approximately every 15 minutes, daily 6am–8pm. Cross-river ferries are available at many points along the river, costing THB4 per crossing.

Longtail boats can also be chartered along both river and canals for around THB500–800 per hour.

Bus. The Bangkok Mass Transit Authority (BMTA; tel: 2246 4262; www.bmta.co.th) operates a large fleet of buses that run along more than 100 established routes all over the city. Fares are THB7–25 per trip depending on how far you're going and the type of bus. BMTA buses are relatively comfortable but slow. Most buses operate daily 5am–11pm but there are also a few all-night buses on certain routes. Bus maps showing the numbered routes are available for purchase at most bookshops in Bangkok.

Metro. The Metropolitan Rapid Transit Authority (MRTA; tel: 0 2246 5733; www.mrta.co.th) operates a subway system that so far offers only one line, the 20km (12½-mile) blue line from Hualamphong Railway Station to Bang Seu Railway Station. Trains operate daily 6am–midnight and fares are THB15–40 depending on distance travelled. Four of the 18 stations connect with the Skytrain.

Skytrain. The BTS Skytrain (tel: 0 2617 7340; www.bts.co.th), an elevated railway with two intersecting lines, is a quick and efficient way to travel across the city. The Sukhumvit Line starts next to Chatuchak Park in northern Bangkok, heads south to the Siam interchange station on Rama I Road and then turns east along Sukhumvit Road near Soi 81. The Silom Line starts at the National Stadium, near Siam Square, heads southwest to Silom and Sathon roads and continues to the foot of Taksin Bridge on the banks of the Chao Phraya River. The city has plans to extend this line over the river into Thonburi. The two lines intersect at Siam Station at Siam Square.

Trains run daily 6am–midnight and fares are THB15–40. One-day (THB120) and three-day (THB310) passes allow unlimited travel.

Taxi. Metered taxis charge THB35 at flagfall for the first 2km (1½ miles), then around THB5 per km. If traffic is moving slowly, a small per-minute surcharge kicks in. If the driver uses a tollway, the passenger pays the charges (THB30–70).

boat	**reua**
bus	**rot meh**
Skytrain	**rot fai faa**
Metro	**rot fai tai din**
taxi	**thaek-see**
Where can I get a taxi?	**Mee rot thaek-see thee nai?**
What's the fare to… ?	**Pai… raakhaa thao rai?**
Where is the bus stop?	**Paai rot meh klai-sut yoo thee nai?**
What time does the next bus to … leave?	**Rot pai… thiaw naa awk kee mohng?**
I want a ticket to…	**Yaak ja seu tua pai…**
single/return	**thiaw diaw/pai klap**
Will you tell me when to get off?	**Khaw bawk wehlaa theung laew?**

R

RELIGION

An estimated 90 percent of Bangkokians profess belief in Theravada Buddhism, the world's oldest and most traditional Buddhist sect. Theravada Buddhists believe that individuals work out their own paths to *nibbana* (nirvana) through a combination of good works, meditation and study of the *dhamma* or Buddhist philosophy. Buddhist monks live ascetic lives in more than 300 monasteries *(wat)* that are dotted around the city.

Around 4 percent of city residents are Muslims, mostly of Malay or Indian descent, and mosques are relatively common in some areas of Bangkok, particularly Bangrak. Many Chinese residents practise Mahayana Buddhism, and there is also a significant number of Sikhs living in the city, along with a sprinkling of Vietnamese and Cambodian Roman Catholics.

T

TELEPHONE

The privately owned, government-subsidised Telephone Organisation of Thailand (TOT) operates land-based telephone services in Thailand. Several GSM-based mobile phone services are available; the most popular are DTAC, Orange, True and AIS. SIM cards may be purchased locally and used with any mobile phone that isn't SIM-locked. Mobile phones and SIM cards with prepaid, short-term accounts may be purchased inexpensively at any department store or mobile phone shop.

The country code for Thailand is 66. Thailand ceased using area codes for different regions in 2003, and all phone numbers now bear eight digits. Add a 0 before to land-line numbers when dialling locally, and 08 before dialling a mobile phone number. If dialling Bangkok from abroad, omit the 0 in both cases.

If dialling abroad from a Bangkok land line, you must dial the international access code 001 before the country code. If dialling from a mobile phone, the international access code is not necessary.

Over half the Thai population now uses mobile phones (with the percentage of mobile usage in Bangkok even higher), hence public phone kiosks are neither as plentiful nor as well maintained as they have been in the past. For the relatively few kiosks that do accept coins nowadays, the 1-baht coin is the standard. More common are phonecard kiosks, which accept cards that can be purchased at any convenience store in denominations ranging from THB25 to THB500.

Hotels usually add surcharges of up to 50 percent over the gazetted phone rates. The least expensive way to call internationally is to use internet phone services, available at most internet cafes.

telephone	**thohrasaap**
long-distance call	**thohrasaap thaan klaai**
international call	**thohrasaap rawaang prateht**
Can you get me this number?	**Khaw mai-lehk thohrasaap nee dai mai**
reverse-charge (collect) call	**thohrasaap kep plaai thaang**
How much per minute?	**Naathee-la raakhaa thao rai?**

TIME DIFFERENCES

Bangkok's time zone is GMT +7 (seven hours ahead of London time) all year. Times are often written using the 24-hour clock (for example, 8pm may be written 2000).

Los Angeles	New York	London	**Bangkok**	Tokyo	Sydney
4am	7am	noon	**7pm**	9pm	10pm

TIPPING

Tipping is never automatic, especially in upmarket hotels and restaurants, where a 10 percent service charge is usually added to the bill. Where there is no service charge, Bangkokians may leave some loose change (no more than THB100) when paying a large restaurant bill. Hotel staff and taxi drivers will appreciate a THB20 per bag tip for luggage assistance, although in neither case is it mandatory.

TOILETS

Most hotels, restaurants and public conveniences have regular sit-down toilets, but cheaper guesthouses may have the more traditional 'squat' toilet. Toilet stalls in most public conveniences are not equipped with toilet paper; you're expected to bring your own tissue or buy some from a vending machine or from staff sitting out front.

toilet (restroom)	**hawng naam**
Where are the toilets?	**Hawng naam yoo thee nai?**

TOURIST INFORMATION

The city government's Bangkok Tourist Division (BTD; 17/1 Phra Athit Road; open Mon–Fri 9am–7pm, Sat–Sun 9am–5pm; tel: 0 2225 7612; www.bangkoktourist.com) has a small office in Banglamphu stocked with free maps, brochures and other useful information on the city. The BTD also maintains counters in Suvarnabhumi Airport, opposite Wat Phra Kaew and at a few shopping centres around the city.

Orientated towards tourism both in Bangkok and the provinces, the Tourist Authority of Thailand (TAT; 1600 New Phetchaburi Road, Makkasan; tel: 0 2250 5500; www.tourismthailand.org) also distributes printed information on Bangkok's sights and culture. There is a second branch in Banghlamphu (Ratchadamnoen Nok Road; open daily 8.30am–4.30pm; tel: 0 2283 1555, ext 1556) adjacent to Ratchadamnoen Boxing Stadium, and information kiosks (open daily 8am–midnight) at Suvarnabhumi and Don Muang airports. The TAT maintains a Tourist Assistance Centre daily 8am–8pm (tel: 1672), outside these hours contact the Tourist Police (tel: 1155).

The TAT operates offices abroad:

Australia: Suite 20, Level 20, 56 Pitt Street, Sydney, NSW 2000; tel: 02 9247 7549; email: info@thailand.net.au.

UK: 1st Floor, 17–19 Cockspur Street, Trafalgar Square, London SW1Y 5BL; tel: 020 7925 2511; email: info@tourismthailand.co.uk. **US:** 61 Broadway, Suite 2810, New York, NY 10006; tel: 212 432 0433; email: tatny@tat.or.th; 1st Floor, 611 North Larchmont Boulevard, Los Angeles, CA 90004; tel: 323 461 9814; email: tatla@ix.netcom.com.

W

WEBSITES AND INTERNET CAFÉS

Internet centres with inexpensive rates (average THB40/hour) are plentiful throughout Bangkok. Many hotels also offer internet connections at much higher rates.

Wi-fi services are expanding rapidly in Bangkok and are widely available in the Silom and Sukhumvit areas. Many coffee shops, including all branches of Starbucks and Au Bon Pain, offer wi-fi access upon purchase of a prepaid card (around THB150/hour). Some coffee shops, such as Coffee Society on Silom Road, offer free wi-fi. Stickman's Guide to Bangkok maintains a useful list of free wi-fi hotspots in the city at www.stickmanbangkok.com/wifi.htm.

Recommended websites for more information on Bangkok include:

www.bangkokpost.com   Bangkok Post newspaper
www.nectec.or.th   National Electronics and Computer Technology Center
www.thaivisa.com/forum   Thai Visa Expat Forum
www.tourismthailand.org   Tourism Authority of Thailand

Y

YOUTH HOSTELS

Bangkok has one member of Hostelling International (www.hihostels.com, the Bangkok International Youth Hostel on Phitsanulok Road. *(See Recommended Hotels on page 134 for details.)*

Recommended Hotels

Hotels are clustered in four main areas: along Silom, Surawong and Sathon roads, Sukhumvit Road between Soi 1 and Soi 33, near Siam Square and Pratunam, and on the banks of the Chao Phraya River. There are also some near the airports. Hundreds of inexpensive guesthouses can be found in the city. It's a good idea to stay near one of the Skytrain lines. Book well in advance, if you plan to arrive during the December–April peak season, especially around Christmas, and in July and August. At other times, there are plenty of rooms available, which may mean lower room rates. Visit www.asiatravel.com and www.res24.com for competitive rates, often cheaper than booking directly.

Larger hotels accept international credit cards, while small hotels and guesthouses will insist on cash. A 10 percent service charge and 7 percent tax are typically added to the room bill for hotels but not for guesthouses. Price guides below are for a standard double room at full rate.

$$$$$	over US$180
$$$$	US$125–180
$$$	US$75–125
$$	US$35–75
$	below US$35

RIVERSIDE

Arun Residence $$$–$$$$ *36–38 Soi Pratoo Nok Yoong, Maharat Road, Ko Ratanakosin, tel: 0 2221 9158, www.arunresidence.com.* Delightful new boutique hotel a couple of minutes' walk from Wat Pho and the Grand Palace, commanding great views over the river towards Wat Arun. The pleasant and comfortable rooms, in a recently renovated Sino-Portugese mansion, are decorated in an elegant contemporary colonial style, and feature all modern amenities. The Deck restaurant *(see page 136)* has great sunset views of Wat Arun.

Ibrik Resort $$$$ *256 Soi Wat Rakang, Arun Amarin Road, Thonburi, tel: 0 2848 9220, www.ibrikresort.com.* A tidy, all-white wooden cottage with only three large rooms and its feet in the river, so that you feel as though you are staying on a riverboat.

Oriental $$$$$ *48 Soi Oriental, Charoen Krung Road, tel: 0 2659 9000, fax: 0 2659 0000, www.mandarinoriental.com/bangkok*. Bangkok's most famous hotel dates back to the late 19th century, and literary figures such as Joseph Conrad and Somerset Maugham have stayed here. The original hotel, now known as the Author's Wing, is dwarfed by two modern high-rise wings added in 1958 and 1976. The hotel's personalised service is legendary, with guest preferences (such as breakfast and reading choices) filed away for future visits. The hotel has its own pier on the Chao Phraya River Express Boat line.

Peninsula $$$$$ *333 Charoen Nakhon Road, tel: 0 2861 2888, fax: 0 2861 1112, www.bangkok.peninsula.com*. Almost directly opposite the Oriental and the Shangri-La, the Peninsula garners more accolades these days than any luxury hotel in Bangkok. Aimed more at the cultured business traveller than the average tourist, the public areas are well decorated, with high-quality contemporary Thai art. Rooms and suites are spacious and well equipped; all come with dazzling river views. The hotel has a private pier with shuttle boats to the Saphan Taksin BTS station and express boat stop.

River View Guest House $ *768 Soi Phanurangsi, Songwat Road, tel: 0 2234 5429, www.riverviewbkk.com*. Wedged between the fancier Silom area and bustling Chinatown, this eight-storey guesthouse is only separated from the Chao Phraya River by a sprawling Chinese temple. Rooms are functional and clean. Views from the inexpensive rooftop restaurant are superb.

SILOM/SURAWONG/SATHON ROADS

Banyan Tree $$$$$ *Thai Wah II Building, 21/100 South Sathon Road, tel: 0 2679 1200, fax: 0 2679 1199, www.banyantree.com*. Ensconced on the lower two and top 28 floors of Bangkok's tallest office building, the Banyan Tree is practically a city in itself. Modern Thai decor prevails, with plenty of jewel-tone silks and woody touches. All rooms have separate sleeping and living areas, and inspiring cityscape views. The world-class spa occupies four adjacent floors, while Vertigo, an open-air bar/restaurant on the rooftop, offers a 360-degree panoramic view.

La Résidence $$$–$$$$ *173/8–9 Surawong Road, tel: 0 2233 3301, www.laresidencebangkok.com.* A boutique hotel with just 26 rooms in a very central location. Some rooms are very tiny but good value, others are more spacious, but all have spic and span bathrooms and a homely atmosphere. Very friendly staff.

Metropolitan $$$$$ *27 South Sathon Road, tel: 0 2625 3333, www. metropolitan.como.bz.* Formerly a YMCA hotel, the Metro has turned a nondescript glass-and-concrete building into a showcase of trendy hotel minimalism. Rooms come with the latest in multimedia gadgetry. On the premises are two fashionable restaurants, Glow and C'yan, the members-only bar Met Bar (guests become automatic members) and the world-class Como Shambala holistic spa.

Sukhothai $$$$$ *13/3 South Sathon Road, tel: 0 2287 0222, fax: 0 2287 4980, www.sukhothai.com.* Architecturally the most uniquely conceived hotel in the capital, the Sukhothai's tribute to postmodern Thai art echoes ancient Buddhist temple architecture with colonnaded exterior corridors and courtyard lily ponds punctuated by *stupas* and Buddha images. Teak-floored rooms are capacious and outfitted with amenities that will satisfy leisure and business travellers alike. The Celadon is one of Bangkok's top hotel-based Thai dining experiences.

Urban Age $ *130/6 Soi 8, Silom Road, tel: 0 2634 2680.* A contemporary version of a favourite backpackers haunt, the Urban Age offers clean but tiny rooms with shared bathrooms, as well as a few dorms. Very well located near the nightspots on Patpong, and run by friendly young Thais.

SIAM SQUARE AND PRATUNAM

Conrad Bangkok $$$$$ *All Seasons Place, 87 Withayu Road, tel: 0 2690 9999, fax: 0 2690 9000, www.conradhotels.com.* Well located in the embassy district off Withayu (Wireless) Road, and within walking distance of the Ploenchit BTS station, the Conrad is aimed at older hipsters with money to appreciate the high life. All rooms and suites come with impressively large and atmospheric bathrooms equipped with flat-screen TVs and sound systems. Off the lobby, the Diplomat Bar is popular with Bangkokians doing business over cocktails. Huge outdoor swimming pool.

Four Seasons Bangkok $$$$$ *155 Ratchadamri Road, tel: 0 2250 1000, fax: 0 2253 9195, www.fourseasons.com.* The public areas of this world-class, business-orientated hotel are tastefully decorated with traditional and modern Thai art, including a striking temple-inspired mural over the massive lobby staircase. Appreciated perks include in-room massages for late-night arrivals and rental vans equipped with computers, cellphones, fax machines and swivelling leather seats for mobile business meetings. Located close to the Rajadamri BTS station.

Grand Hyatt Erawan $$$$$ *494 Ratchadamri Road, tel: 0 2254 1234, fax: 0 2254 6308, www.bangkok.hyatt.com.* Grandly executed neoclassical Thai architecture is the hallmark of the Grand Hyatt Erawan, along with the world's largest rotating collection of modern Thai art. Rooms at the back overlook the grassy turf of the Bangkok Royal Sports Club race track while most other rooms face adjacent buildings. The relatively new i.sawan residential spa on an intermediate rooftop offers private treatment bungalows, a huge fitness centre, a swimming pool, and treatments that draw from traditional Thai medicine as well as modern spa technology.

Holiday Mansion $$ *53 Withayu Road at Ploenchit Road, tel: 0 2255 0099, fax: 0 2253 0130.* This efficiently run upper budget-range hotel occupies a prime position opposite the UK embassy and next to the Ploenchit BTS station. Recently renovated rooms are huge. A swimming pool, massage centre and two restaurants, one Italian and one Thai, on the ground floor.

Reno Hotel $$ *40 Soi Kasem San 1, Rama I Road, tel: 0 2215 0026, fax: 0 2215 3430, www.renohotel.co.th.* Opposite the National Stadium and near the National Stadium BTS station, this veteran of the Vietnam War R&R scene has been refurbished into a smart budget hotel with a near-chic lobby, a swimming pool and excellent late-night coffee shop.

Siam@Siam $$$$ *865 Phra Rama I Road, tel: 0 2217 3000, www.siamatsiam.com.* A bright and contemporary hotel on the 14th–25th floors of a skyscaper, featuring industrial design elements such as polished concrete and railway sleepers, as well as lots of wood and some splashes of colour. The rooms have superb views over the city centre and the National Stadium. The hotel features an excellent spa, a popular bar and good restaurants.

Swissôtel Nai Lert Park $$$$$ *2 Withayu Road, tel: 0 2253 0123, fax: 0 2253 6509, www.swissotel.com/bangkok-nailertpark.* Surrounded by generously landscaped gardens and ponds, the Swissôtel Nai Lert Park offers a calm, near-bucolic retreat from gritty urban Bangkok. A large new wing with retro 1970s furnishings has upped the hotel's chic factor. The lobby lounge hosts jazz nightly. As befits Bangkok hotels built before the 1980s boom decade, rooms tend to be spacious, and all have been updated to include the latest in bathroom and business hotel technology.

SUKHUMVIT ROAD

Atlanta $ *78 Soi 2 (Soi Phasak), Sukhumvit Road, tel: 0 2252 6069, fax: 0 2656 8123, www.theatlantahotelbangkok.com.* Opened in the 1950s as the private Atlanta Club, this ageing seven-storey hotel is a favourite choice among budget travellers who wish to avoid crowded Banglamphu. Rooms and suites come in several sizes and price ranges, and as the quality varies, it's best to have a look before you select a room. Although only a stone's throw from the Nana red-light district, the Atlanta enforces a strict policy barring the sex trade from the premises. The period-perfect lobby and tropical-landscaped pool turn up frequently in locally produced films and TV dramas.

Davis $$$$ *Soi 24, Sukhumvit Road, tel: 0 2260 8000, www.davisbangkok.net.* Eclecticism is the name of the game at the Davis, where every room is decorated with a different theme, from French to Zen. In addition to over 200 rooms, there are 10 two- and three-bedroom Thai-style villas that offer the ultimate in space and privacy, with individual lap pools and gardens. Shopping at the Emporium is close at hand, as is the Phrom Phong BTS.

Federal Hotel $–$$ *27 Soi 11, Sukhumvit Road, tel: 0 2253 0175, www.federalbangkok.com.* A stable fixture on the Sukhumvit Road hotel scene for a long while, the Vietnam War-era 'Fed' attracts repeat visitors with its affordable rates, location near the Asoke BTS station and large and inexpensive American-style coffee shop. The minuscule pool isn't large enough for laps but good for cooling off.

JW Marriott $$$$$ *4 Sukhumvit Road at Soi 2, tel: 0 2656 7700, fax: 0 2656 7711, www.jwmarriott.com.* The most luxurious hotel on Sukhumvit Road, the JW Marriott is a top choice among business travellers for its comfortably sleek lobby lounge, well-decorated rooms, state-of-the-art fitness centre and convenient location near the Nana BTS station. Tsu-Nami, a Japanese restaurant on the bottom floor, is locally renowned for sushi.

Ma Du Zi $$$$$ *corner of Ratchadapisek Road and Sukhumvit Soi 16, tel: 0 2615 6400, www.maduzihotel.com.* Ma Du Zi means 'come and see' and this super-luxurious hotel definitely deserves to be seen for its excellent design. The 40 or so rooms are large, decorated with lots of wood, marble and sumptuous textiles, and each comes with with a printer, espresso machine and contemporary art work. The hotel has a well reputed French restaurant.

Seven $$$$ *3/15 Soi 31, Sukhumvit Road, tel: 0 2662 0951, www.sleepatseven.com.* Seven has six rooms and a communal lounge/bar/gallery space, each decorated in a different colour, inspired by the deep-rooted Thai belief that each day of the week has its own colour, reflecting a specific god. This home away from home has a very contemporary feel, but is very Thai at the same time, attracting a young, trendy crowd. Rooms are well equipped and come with free mobile phones.

BANGLAMPHU AND THEWET

Bangkok International Youth Hostel $ *25/2 Phitsanulok Road, tel: 0 2282 0950, www.hihostels.com.* Thailand's oldest hostel occupies a multi-storey building and offers both inexpensive dorm accommodation and private rooms.

Boworn BB $ *335 Phra Sumen Road, tel: 0 2629 1073.* Small, friendly guesthouse with clean but basic rooms, well away from the main Khao San tourist drag. Excellent home-cooked curries are served in the rooftop cafe.

Buddy Lodge $$ *265 Khao San Road, tel: 0 2629 4477, www. buddylodge.com.* Khao San Road's nicest accommodation contains comfortable rooms with white-painted wood-and-brass decor hinting at early 20th-century Bangkok. The hotel offers something for everyone in its ground-floor complex, including a coffee shop/bookshop and a tattoo and piercing parlour.

Hotel De'Moc (Thai Hotel) $–$$ *78 Prachatipatai Road, tel: 0 2282 2831, fax: 0 2280 1299, www.hoteldemoc.com.* Built in 1962 and until recently known as Thai Hotel, the De'Moc (named after the Democracy Monument a few streets away) is a reliable two-star hotel with 100 plain but comfortable rooms, a swimming pool and a better-than-average travel agency.

Old Bangkok Inn $$$ *609 Phra Sumen Road, tel: 0 2629 1787, www.oldbangkokinn.com.* This former Banglamphu shop-house has a new life as a budget bed and breakfast dedicated to 'green' practices. The six sumptuously painted suites each have a Thai herb or flower theme, from lemongrass to jasmine.

Phranakorn Nornlen $$–$$$ *46 Thewet Soi 1, Krung Kasem Road, tel: 0 2628 8188, www.phranakorn-nornlen.com.* Small but utterly charming and award-winning hotel in a wooden house with a peaceful courtyard. The rooms are comfortable and quiet, there is plenty of communal space, including a library/living room and a rooftop garden where the staff grows their own organic vegetables.

Royal Hotel $$ *Ratchadamnoen Klang Road at Atsadang Road, tel: 0 2222 9111-26, fax: 0 2224 2083.* Bangkok's third-oldest hotel stands within walking distance of Wat Phra Kaew and Wat Pho. Rooms in the old wing are larger than those in the new wing. The 24-hour coffee shop is a favourite rendezvous for local Thais.

Shanti Lodge $ *37 Soi Thewet, Si Ayuthaya Road, tel: 0 2281 2497.* Near the National Library and close to the Chao Phraya River, this long-running guesthouse blends Thai and Santa Fe decor to create a cosy atmosphere. Vegetarians will enjoy the open-air café, which is known for its veggie fare.

Tuptim Bed & Breakfast $ *82 Rambutri Road, tel: 0 2629 1535, www.tuptimb-b.com.* The latest trend in Banglamphu is to restore old wooden homes and turn them into boutique-style guesthouses. Here the 25 rooms are simply furnished in what might be called 'country Bangkok' style. Separate, gender-segregated bathrooms are well maintained. Popular authentic Thai restaurant.

Viengtai Hotel $$ *42 Rambutri Road, tel: 0 2280 5434, www.viengtai.co.th.* Although dated in design, art and furnishings, the venerable Viengtai makes a peaceful retreat amid the hustle and bustle of Khao San Road close by. Friendly and efficient staff. Good travel agency and a swimming pool.

AIRPORTS

Amari Don Muang Hotel $$$$ *333 Choet Wutthakat Road, tel: 0 2566 1020, fax: 0 2566 1941, www.amari.com.* Opposite Don Muang Airport and accessible via an enclosed footbridge, the Amari is the hotel of choice in the Don Muang area. It has over 300 rooms and suites, each stocked with international-class amenities.

Novotel Suvarnabhumi Airport $$$ *999 Suvarnabhumi Airport Hotel Mu 1, Samut Prakan, tel: 0 2131 1111, fax: 0 2131 1188, www.novotelsuvarnabhumi.com.* A new 600-room hotel offering free 24-hour shuttle vans to the airport, a swimming pool, a de luxe spa, four restaurants and bars, plus a fitness centre.

Recommended Restaurants

Bangkok's eating choices cover virtually all Asian and most Western cuisines. As the epicentre for all things Thai, naturally it's Thai food that Bangkok does best. Choice of ambience varies from humble noodle carts to five-star luxury hotel restaurants and dinner river cruises.

The restaurants listed here are arranged alphabetically by district, following roughly the same scheme as Recommended Hotels. In general, the most expensive restaurants are in the Silom and Sukhumvit areas, although even here you can find budget gems catering to local residents. Banglamphu has become one of the city's latest epicentres for Thai food culture.

On the whole, the cost of eating out in Bangkok is relatively low compared to most capital cities. Price ranges given below are rough guides only, based on an three-course meal for one, without drinks (alcoholic beverages can raise the bill significantly) or tips. Advance reservations are rarely necessary in Bangkok – indeed, most non-hotel restaurants do not accept them – except in the peak December–January season when the most popular upmarket tourist restaurants may fill up early.

$$$$	over US$30
$$$	US$20–30
$$	US$10–20
$	below US$10

RIVERSIDE

Deck $$$ *Arun Residence, 36–38 Soi Pratoo Nok Yoong, Maharat Road, Ko Ratanakosin, tel: 0 2221 9158*. In a great river location, near Wat Pho, this restaurant is the best place to watch the sun set behind Wat Arun. It has a small but delicious menu of Thai specials.

Kaolang Home Kitchen $$ *2 Si Ayuthaya Road, Thewet, tel: 0 2281 9228*. Hard to find on a rambling wooden deck overlooking the river, but worth the search, Kaolang Home Kitchen specialises in fresh seafood and fish. The atmosphere is totally relaxed and the food is wonderful and fresh. It's is the perfect place for a long, leisurely meal of *tom yam* (prawn and lemongrass soup), *phat phak bung fai daeng* (water spinach flash-fried in bean sauce, garlic and chillies) and cold beer.

Supatra River House $$$ *266 Soi Wat Rakhang, Thonburi, tel: 0 2411 0305, www.supatrariverhouse.net*. The location of this converted Thai villa has wonderful views of Wat Phra Kaew and Wat Arun on either side of the river, which are impressive when illuminated at night. The menu is for the most part traditional Thai, although some dishes, such as *tom som salmon* (salmon steamed in sour soup), have been given a contemporary spin. A free ferry service to the restaurant is available from Tha Mahathat Pier.

Ton Pho $ *43 Phra Athit Road, tel: 0 2280 0452*. A rambling wooden-floored, open-air dining hall at the river's edge is the scene for authentic old-school Thai cooking, with an emphasis on delicious, fresh seafood.

Yok Yor Marina $$ *Soi Somdet Chao Phraya 17, Thonburi, tel: 0 2863 0565, www.yokyor.co.th*. Opposite the River City shopping complex, this huge open-air complex is one of several Yok Yor branches. The *haw mok* (fish steamed in banana leaves with curry paste) is highly recommended. Patrons can choose to board the nightly 8pm dinner cruise boat for a small surcharge.

SILOM/SURAWONG/SATHON ROADS

Blue Elephant $$$$ *233 South Sathon Road, tel: 0 2673 9353, www.blueelephant.com*. This Belgian- and Thai-owned enterprise originated in Brussels over 20 years ago and now has branches in nine locales around the world. Housed in the stately Sino-Portuguese, former Chinese-Thai Chamber of Commerce, the elegant restaurant specialises in royal Thai cuisine with occasional fusion touches. The Blue Elephant's cooking school is highly respected.

Eat Me $$$ *Soi Phiphat 2, off Convent Road, Silom, tel: 0 2238 0931, www.eatmerestaurant.com*. Chic and elegant Australian-owned restaurant serving a fusion menu that makes a welcome change from spicy Thai food. The dishes are tasty, inventive and beautifully served. It's always busy, so book ahead.

Harmonique $$ *34 Soi 24, Charoen Krung Road, tel: 0 2237 8175.* A round-doored former Chinese residence near the main post office is the setting for this cosy getaway from busy Charoen Krung Road. Well-prepared Thai and Chinese dishes are served at Hokkien-style marble-topped tables.

Indian Hut $$ *311/2–5 Surawong Road, tel: 0 2635 7876, www. indianhut-bangkok.com.* Up three flights of stairs above Surawong Road shops, Indian Hut is a rarity in that the kitchen focuses on Nawabi (Lucknow) cuisine, both vegetarian and non-vegetarian. The prawns cooked in ginger are a house speciality.

Khrua Aroy Aroy $ *Pan Road, off Silom Road, tel: 0 2635 2365.* This traditional Thai eatery opposite Wat Maha Uma Devi displays the day's curries and soups in a row of large pots. Of particular note is the *khanom jeen yaa* (thin rice noodles ladled with fish curry) and *thawt man plaa* (fried fishcakes with peanut-cucumber sauce). Lunchtime is the best time to visit, though it's open until 9pm.

Mizu's Kitchen $$ *Soi Patpong 1, tel: 0 2233 6447.* A Patpong fixture since the Indochina War era, Mizu's has a loyal Japanese and Thai following for its steak and Americanised Japanese fare.

Soi Polo Fried Chicken $ *137/1–3 Soi Polo, Withayu Road, tel: 0 1252 2252.* A legend among local office workers and embassy staff, Soi Polo Fried Chicken specialises in Isan (northeastern Thai) cuisine, which means in addition to their signature garlic-heaped fried chicken (possibly Bangkok's best), the cooks also prepare delicious *somtam* (spicy green papaya salad), *laap* (sautéed minced chicken or duck in savoury herbs and spices) and other standard Isan dishes.

Thip Samai Phat Thai $ *313 Mahachai Road, tel: 0 2221 6280.* This humble street-side vendor near the Democracy Monument has been serving Bangkok's finest *phat thai* (literally 'Thai-fried' – slender rice noodles stir-fried with tofu, bean sprouts, peanuts and prawns) for over 40 years. Choose among seven kinds of *phat thai*, including the house version, combining fresh prawns, fresh crab, prawn roe, squid and sliced green mango. Try the delicious freshly squeezed orange juice or frozen coconut juice.

SIAM SQUARE AND PRATUNAM

Café Lenôtre $$$ *Natural Ville Executive Residences, 61 Soi Lang Suan, tel: 0 2250 7050.* A branch of the famous Parisian café-restaurant chain, Café Lenôtre combines some of the highlights of French cuisine – a patisserie, chocolatier, boulanger and bistro – all in one. Fixed-price meals including an appetiser, main course and dessert are good value.

Gianni's Ristorante $$$ *34/1 Soi Tonson, off Ploenchit Road, tel: 0 2252 1619, www.giannibkk.com.* This extremely popular Italian restaurant deserves advance reservations. The vast menu provides Italian favourites cooked to perfection, and the wine list is one of Bangkok's best non-hotel offerings. House specialities include lobster-stuffed ravioli.

Nguan Lee Lang Suan $ *Corner of Soi Lang Suan and Soi Sarasin, tel: 0 2250 0936.* This semi-outdoor place specialising in Chinese-style seafood is open until 3am and popular with local clubbers for its traditional home cooking and quick service.

SUKHUMVIT ROAD

Bed Supperclub $$$$ *26 Soi 11, Sukhumvit Road, tel: 0 2651 3537.* As famous for its space-age looks as its food, Bed is named after the huge bed-like sofas where diners lounge and nibble from low tray-tables. DJs spin chill-out mixes as white-clad table attendants glide between floors, yet despite the novelty impression, the East-West fusion cuisine is among the best Bangkok offers.

Bourbon St Bar & Restaurant $$$ *Soi 22, Sukhumvit Road, tel: 0 2259 0328, www.bourbonstbkk.com.* This New Orleans-themed dining room, a favourite with Bangkok expatriates, offers relatively authentic Cajun and Creole cooking, along with a few Mexican dishes. Some nights there is also free live music.

Crêpes & Co. $$$ *18/1 Soi 12, Sukhumvit Road, tel: 0 2653 3990.* As the name suggests, this French-owned restaurant serves high-quality crêpes of all kinds, along with European-style breakfasts, and an admirable selection of Mediterranean, Moroccan and Spanish lunch and dinner specialities.

Face $$$ *29 Soi 38, Sukhumvit Road, tel: 0 2713 6048, www.face bars.com.* Three delightful restaurants in one, set in connected wooden Thai houses. Lan Na Thai serves great Thai specialities, Hazara specialises in a flavoursome North Indian cuisine, while Visage, the bakery, serves arguably the best pastries and cakes in town.

Imoya $$ *3rd floor, Terminal Shop Cabin, 2/17–19 Soi 24, Sukhumvit Road, tel: 0 2663 5185.* An old-fashioned Japanese restaurant with wood-panelling, sake and good Japanese dishes.

Khrua Rommai $ *16 Soi 36, Sukhumvit Road, tel: 0 2661 2340.* Housed in a private home and plant-filled garden, this family-owned restaurant serves both Thai and Lao cuisines. Specialities include *phat krathiam kung* (prawn stir-fried with garlic).

Kuppa $$ *39 Soi 16, Sukhumvit Road, tel: 0 2663 0450.* Long fashionable with both Thais and expats, Kuppa is famous for its excellent pastries, breakfasts, pastas, pizzas and strong fresh coffee.

Le Dalat $$ *47/1 Soi 23, Sukhumvit Road, tel: 0 2258 4192.* An elegant oasis in busy Central Bangkok, this restaurant has the city's most celebrated Vietnamese menu. *Naem meuang* (grilled meatballs wrapped in lettuce leaves with steamed rice-flour wrappers, garlic, chilli, ginger, starfruit, mango and tamarind sauce) is the house speciality.

Maha Naga $$$$ *Soi 29, Sukhumvit Road, tel: 0 2662 3060.* Amid a fantasy-like blend of Asian and Moroccan design motifs and courtyard fountains, the relatively new Maha Naga strives to outdo the rest of the city in its Thai-Continental fusions.

Mrs Balbir's $$ *155/1–2 Soi 11/1, Sukhumvit Road, tel: 0 2651 0498, www.mrsbalbir.com*. Family-style Indian cuisine, designed to please Thai, Western and Indian palates, is served in this restaurant near the Swiss Park Hotel. Mrs Balbir is a local celebrity with her own TV cooking show. She runs Indian cooking lessons on the mezzanine level of her restaurant.

Rang Mahal $$$ *Rembrandt Hotel, Soi 18, Sukhumvit Road, tel: 0 2261 7100*. Perched on the top floor of this mid-range hotel, Rang Mahal is Bangkok's most elegant Indian restaurant. The menu offers both North and South Indian cuisines, enhanced by attentive service and the opportunity for spectacular cityscape views from an adjacent open-air observation platform.

Tamarind Café $$ *27 Soi 20, Sukhumvit Road, tel: 0 2663 7421, www.tamarind-cafe.com*. This hip three-storey café and gallery is a local favourite for its light Asian vegetarian fare and rotating photography exhibits.

Thonglee $$ *Soi 20, Sukhumvit Road, tel: 0 2258 1983*. Popular traditional Thai restaurant with no frills at all – decor includes a large house shrine and plastic table cloths – but the food is authentic, including the delicious *mee krawp* (sweet and spicy crispy noodles).

Vientiane Kitchen $ *8 Soi 36, Sukhumvit Road, tel: 0 2258 6171*. Bangkok's most casual and popular restaurant offers fiery Lao-Isan favourites such as *kai yaang* (spicy grilled chicken), *laap* (spicy minced-meat salad) and *som-tam* (green papaya salad). The Lao-Isan decor is supplemented by a live band playing *maw lam* (traditional Lao-Isan folk music).

BANGLAMPHU AND THE WET

Baan Phra Arthit $ *102/1 Phra Athit Road, tel: 02280 7878*. A good place for lunch or afternoon relaxing, this air-conditioned café is more stylish than most. Good coffee and cakes, and a small selection of Western and Thai standard dishes are served in a pleasant atmosphere.

Chote Chitr $ *146 Phraeng Phuton Road, tel: 0 2221 4082.* Classic Thai cuisine is the forte here. Recipes that are slowly disappearing elsewhere in Bangkok, such as *mee krawp* (crisp-fried rice noodles in coconut sauce) and *yam hua phlee* (banana-flower salad), are well preserved at Chote Chitr.

Jey Hoy $ *Soi 2, Samsen Road.* A brisk walk from Khao San Road, this venerated corner spot is so cramped most diners sit at tables along the pavement. The best dishes here make use of fresh clams, crab and other seafood, prepared Thai- and Hokkien-style.

Khrua Nopparat $ *136 Phra Athit Road, tel: 0 2281 7578.* In an area that is being gradually gentrified, Khrua Nopparat maintains the same fluorescent-lit, no-puffery decor standards that it has done for 20 years. The bilingual menu displays all the standard Thai soups and curries. You can also ask to try some of the rotating house recommendations.

Kuay Tiaw Mae $ *Phra Athit Road.* This inexpensive noodle house serves traditional Thai rice noodle dishes, including the incendiary but delightful *kuaytiaw tom yam* (rice noodles in a chilli-laden lemongrass broth).

Roti-Mataba $ *Corner of Phra Athit and Phra Sumen roads.* Opposite Santichaiprakan Park, this narrow two-storey restaurant serves excellent southern Thai-style curries with *roti*, an Indian-influenced flatbread wrap. Rice dishes are also available. The upstairs dining room is air-conditioned, the downstairs is alfresco.

Vijit $$ *Democracy Monument roundabout, Ratchadamnoen Klang Road, tel: 0 282 0958.* The air of faded elegance at this classic Thai restaurant appears to go down well with the clientele, mainly staff from local government offices. Everything on the menu is authentically prepared, especially the *yam* (spicy Thai-style salads).

Berlitz pocket guide

Bangkok

Second Edition 2010

Written by Joe Cummings
Updated by Sylvie Franquet
Edited by Anna Tyler
Series Editor: Tony Halliday

Printed in Singapore by Insight Print Services (Pte) Ltd, 38 Joo Koon Road, Singapore 628990. Tel: (65) 6865-1600. Fax: (65) 6861-6438

Berlitz Trademark Reg. U.S. Patent Office and other countries. Marca Registrada

Photography credits
Francis Dorai 1, 40–1, 42, 52, 67; Jason Lang 3, 9, 22, 46, 50, 51, 55, 60, 61, 62, 73, 74, 75, 76, 79, 80, 82, 84, 87, 93, 100, 103, 104; M.C. Piya Rangsit 18; Travis Rowan/Alamy 99; Luca Tettoni 15, 34; Marcus Wislon Smith 6, 8, 10, 11, 13, 16, 24, 27, 28, 29, 30, 32, 33, 35, 36, 38, 39, 47, 49, 56, 57, 63, 64, 66, 70, 71, 89, 90, 94, 96; Rungroj Yongrit/epa/Corbis 21.

Cover picture: 4Corners Images

Every effort has been made to provide accurate information in this publication, but changes are inevitable. The publisher cannot be responsible for any resulting loss, inconvenience or injury.

Contact us

At Berlitz we strive to keep our guides as accurate and up to date as possible, but if you find anything that has changed, or if you have any suggestions on ways to improve this guide, then we would be delighted to hear from you.

Berlitz Publishing, PO Box 7910,
London SE1 1WE, England.
fax: (44) 20 7403 0290
email: berlitz@apaguide.co.uk
www.berlitzpublishing.com